BRICK WALLS

Tales of Hope & Courage from Pakistan

BRICK WALLS

Tales of Hope & Courage from Pakistan

Saadia Faruqi

FB PUBLISHING
SAN CLEMENTE

Published by:

FB Publishing
645 Camino De Los Mares
Suite 108-276
San Clemente, CA 92673
Visit our website at www.fbpublishinghouse.com

Cover design: Susan Veach
Book Design: Daniel Middleton | www.scribefreelance.com

ISBN: 978-0-9903876-6-4

First Edition

Printed in the United States of America

To My Father

Introduction

In the last few years, the War on Terror has refocused the world's attention from Iraq and Afghanistan to the northwestern hills and southern plains of Pakistan. Media reports from that country range from violent to pitiful, and most westerners think of it either as a haven for extremists or a prison for women and minorities. We hear daily about drone attacks, blasphemy laws, inequality, and injustice. Yet, little is known about Pakistan's rich culture or colorful daily life. Nobody seems to know or care to discuss the strides being taken in education, social services, and even politics that are improving the nation every year. It's probably not newsworthy.

As my country of birth, where I resided until my early twenties, Pakistan holds a special place in my heart despite the challenges it presents. Yes, the poverty is deplorable, the politicians are corrupt, and religious strife is troubling. But it is also a nation full of kind-hearted individuals struggling to make their society better with optimism and resolve. That's the Pakistan I want people to know about: a nation of millions working hard during the day, watching television late at night, drinking tea, talking politics, playing cricket on weekends, loving their families, and worshipping God every day. From the aid workers to the local anonymous donors, from people with nothing in their pockets to those blessed with abundance, I have seen my fellow countrymen and women help each other in ways that revive my confidence in human nature.

The inspiration for this collection came to me after my father's death in 2012 when I visited my family home in Karachi and met or heard about dozens of people – poor widows, illiterate young children, random strangers on the street – whom he had helped with money and advice over his lifetime. My father was not a rich man, and he struggled with serious illnesses from a young age. Despite these obstacles, he continued to assist those less fortunate in ways I had no knowledge about until after he died. He put some children through school, and paid for others' textbooks. He assisted servants in building their first homes and poor relatives in collecting dowries for their daughters' weddings. He helped many strangers find jobs and guided many others in financial and professional decisions. Apart from my mother, nobody else knew about his generosity. He really lived the mantra of not letting the left hand know what the right hand was doing. Listening to the stories of the people he had helped over the years made me realize that he couldn't have been alone. There must be so many others like him who willingly share some of the burden of their neighbors, but never seek recognition or acknowledgement.

This collection of short stories is dedicated with gratitude to my father and other Pakistanis like him. It describes the brick walls people face, challenges to happiness and prosperity. The characters are fictional but their situations are based on metaphorical walls, unique struggles created by the exceptional culture and environment that is Pakistan. Some brick walls come in the form of human beings, others through ideologies or stereotypes. Walls can be events or accidents; they can even be preconceived notions in one's own mind that form a roadblock to moving forward. Pakistanis face these brick walls every day, and how they surmount them is called "life". I can't join them in their struggles. I can only tell their stories.

—Saadia Faruqi

Angel of Hope

Asma was late. As she hurried down the uneven brick path, past the rows of decaying houses with laundry blowing in the light breeze and satellite receivers jostling for attention, she wished for the thousandth time that she could afford a watch. She really didn't desire an expensive watch, like the one her neighbor Sameena had received from her fiancé in Dubai. Any old watch would do so that she could tell when it was time to leave for work. For work was more than a livelihood; it was a lifeline Asma couldn't do without.

Out of the corner of her eye she saw Sameena looking out of the window. The light of the sun glinted off the new watch in question. If she's not careful someone's going to steal that right off her wrist, thought Asma unkindly. Sameena waved, and Asma immediately felt ashamed of her thoughts. "I'll be back soon. Thank you for keeping an eye on Nabeel," she called out as she walked towards the street corner. At the words, a small head poked out from behind the single brown curtain, eyes bleary, face flushed red, attempting a valiant smile despite the runny nose. Her poor Nabeel, six years old, was sick with fever and crying to snuggle with his mama. Her heart broke to leave him, but the separation would be temporary, *Inshallah.* Sameena lived next door and had promised to stay with him until Asma returned in the evening.

The street was littered with trash that women had thrown out of their homes. Asma sidestepped rotting fruit and thanked Allah that the garbage man hadn't come yet to set the trash on fire. It made the whole street stink and her clothes smell of smoke. "Seems like the garbage man doesn't have a watch either," she mused. After all, watches were luxuries that she and others like her only dreamed about.

Her old watch, given to her by her father as a wedding present, had fallen off a shelf and broken into pieces several weeks ago. Sentimental value aside, its loss in her life's routine was monumental. She added it to the mental list of things she would buy when she finally had some money. Asma called this mental list her "angel list", because she truly believed that nothing short of a miracle brought to her by an angel of heaven would allow her to be free of the crippling poverty she was living in. This too, was more of a private joke than anything else. Although she believed in angels, the thought of one answering her prayers for a better life and a brighter future seemed quite farfetched. Things like that only happened in the stories she remembered from her childhood.

Asma heaved a sigh. Sometimes she wished she could go back in time to being a little girl again. She had always been poor, she reflected, as she reached the bus stop at the corner of her street, but recently it seemed that she was becoming more and more dissatisfied with her lot in life. Her parents, now long dead, had worked hard in small jobs all their lives, never making enough to rest easy. Her father taught the Quran to children in their neighborhood and her mother sewed clothes; income was little but steady. They had virtually no conveniences, but her childhood had been filled with laughter and lots of bedtime stories that allowed her to imagine anything, everything. Those were the good days, when it was safe to play in the street, women were respected, and everyone helped each other.

Now things were different. The country was less safe, people were more violent. And she was no longer an innocent child who could count on the protection of her parents. She was an adult, poor, and at twenty eight years, a widow. The mere idea of an angel to the rescue was laughable, yet for some reason she was wishing it more and more these past few months. She wondered why. Was it her sense of desperation or a feeling of hopelessness that prompted her to hide in a dream world?

Hunger pangs shook her out of her deliberations and she realized that she hadn't eaten since the night before. She reached in her threadbare bag and took out a banana. It was soft and brown, but it was all she had. She had just started peeling it when she saw a movement beside her. An emaciated child, barefoot and in torn clothing stood next to her, gazing longingly at the banana. "No," she declared, awarding him the strongest glare she could manage. "I am not giving this to you. Go beg somewhere else. Don't you know that begging is a sin?"

There was no response from the child. She fumed silently. She tried to ignore him, but he remained steadfastly at her side, eyes pleading. He couldn't be any older than Nabeel. Finally with a frustrated sigh she handed the banana to him. "Here, I hope you're happy. Now I'm going to be hungry, thanks to you." He broke into a crooked smile, snatched the banana out of her hand before she could change her mind, and ran away. She gazed at him furiously, already regretting her decision.

Asma was brought out of her thoughts by a loud rattling sound on the street, accompanied by a deafening roar and blaring Urdu music. She saw the bus rambling slowly and noisily towards her and she felt anger rising again. Why couldn't the bus driver drive any faster? Surely he had to know that the crowd of people waiting at the stop all had somewhere to go? Nobody would ride in a dangerously overcrowded old bus just to pass their time, would they? She decided to give the driver a harsh talking to when he arrived, but the rush of people shoving to get inside made her forgive and forget. She joined the surge entering the bus, delivering as many elbows as she received.

The bus ride was suffocating and long, and she felt the absence of her watch sorely. She looked around in desperation. The woman squeezed beside her on the hard bench was wearing a watch. Asma tried to angle her face to see the time, but a few attempts left her feeling cross-eyed and the watch owner suspicious. "What are you looking at?" demanded the woman, her wizened face marked with age and exhaustion.

"I'm sorry. I just wanted to know the time." Asma was duly apologetic, but her words fell on deaf ears. The woman obviously thought her a potential thief, for she promptly removed the watch from her wrist and put it into her purse. Asma would have felt offended if the move hadn't allowed her to glimpse the face of the watch as it disappeared into the purse. Her purpose had been achieved and she was seized with a bigger worry than a rude fellow passenger. The time was now 10:05 a.m.... she was already five minutes late and she still had some traveling to do.

Asma wasn't devout but it seemed as if praying had recently become her last resort more times than she cared to remember. She spent the rest of the ride praying for the bus to go faster, for time to stand still, for anything to delay the inevitable. But, as usual, Allah seemed to be unaware of her plight.

The bus finally rolled to a stop and she descended hastily, elbowing her way out in the same way she had pushed in. She had finally arrived in Karachi's busy city center Saddar, where new businesses jostled for space alongside old cathedrals and catholic schools left behind from the colonial era. Business was always booming which meant that her boss, master tailor Akbar, opened promptly at 10 o'clock in the morning. How ironic that in a nation seemingly devoid of commitment or punctuality, her place of work always opened right on time. This is why I need a watch, she lamented to herself yet again as she approached the shop with heavy feet.

Akbar was waiting outside, a look of palpable annoyance on his face. He was a tall man with a receding hairline and perpetually stern features, and Asma was slightly afraid of him. More than Allah, it was this man who held her life and livelihood in his hands, but without a care of his precious burden. When he saw her, he erupted. "Where have you been? You are more than half an hour late!"

"I'm so sorry, my son is sick and I broke my watch and my home is so far away..." Asma realized she was rambling but she couldn't help it. She could see from his expression that this time he wasn't going to listen to her excuses. She braced herself for the worst, and was surprised when he swatted away her explanations and motioned her inside impatiently.

"Mrs. Malik is coming for her clothes at noon. They need to be ready by that time," he said. "I'm giving you one last chance, you hear me? You know that we can't afford to disappoint this customer. But remember, one more mistake and I will take great pleasure in kicking you out!"

Asma couldn't believe he wasn't firing her on the spot. This wasn't the first time she was late, but she had been sure this was going to be the last. Perhaps someone was listening to her prayers after all. She hurried into the shop and to her station as the other three employees avoided her gaze. It was a cramped space, with piles of fabric in varying stages of completion heaped behind the rickety old sewing machine tables. Her mother had taught her to sew, and while Asma was grateful, it was becoming more and more obvious to her that she was sorely lacking in skill. She could sew a simple *shalwar kameez* but anything more elaborate became a challenging task. Women these days wanted intricate designing and handiwork on their clothes and Akbar needed someone who was able to satisfy the endless requests of his customers.

Her colleagues in the shop knew this as well, for it was a frequent topic of discussion as they worked for long hours hunched over their sewing machines. Aisha, the oldest and most experienced seamstress, was the resident mother hen. Despite her greying hair and bad breath, she lost no opportunity to inform Asma how superior her craft was. Mahvish, with her ever-present sparkly bangles and made-up face was about Asma's own age, but happily married with a brood of children. Her husband had a stable job washing dishes in a Chinese restaurant, a fact that she never failed to mention in any conversation, for an employed and responsible husband was indeed a gem for women of their status. Jamal was still a teenager, with oily, slicked-back hair and earphones blasting the latest Indian film music into his ears. Despite his uncaring attitude, Asma had a soft spot for him, imagining often that her own Nabeel would be a younger version of Jamal in a few years' time. She couldn't wait for the time to fly and her pride and joy to become a young man. Jamal, though, was another matter. As the sewing ladies' assistant, he was in charge of the enormous iron used to press fabric they needed, or clothes they completed. Despite his lowly position, he had a secret weapon: he was also Akbar's nephew and hence often careless of his duties. After all, who was going to report him to Akbar?

Asma would have loved to hate them all, and at times she did, but relationships within the shop were complicated. Working eight hours every day in such cramped quarters didn't allow for hatred to flourish. They depended on each other, their jobs often more of an assembly line than individual projects. Akbar bought huge rolls of silks, satins, cottons and laces from the wholesale market every week and often customers brought their own fabric for sewing as well. Once Jamal finished ironing each piece of cloth, Aisha would cut it into shape, carefully and with great flourish, because they all knew how important the right cut was. Then Mahvish would take one part to sew the long tunic or *kameez*, and Asma would start on the loose pants or *shalwar*. Although they were all kind to her, they knew in their hearts that sewing the *shalwar* was the easiest. Mahvish and Aisha would collaborate on the sketching, designing, and finally the joining of an array of multi colored fabrics and laces together to create a beautiful, frothy *kameez*. The *shalwar* – or sometimes the straight pant that was becoming fashionable now – was by comparison an artless, humble accompaniment that gave testimony to Asma's lack of skill.

Asma dreamed of becoming an expert seamstress like Aisha, a dream that had lately started consuming her with a passion. Aisha had studied her craft in a special sewing school and she liked nothing better than to boast about her superior training. Knowing Asma needed some help, she had kindly promised to talk to the principal about admission. Asma didn't think it polite to refuse, although in her heart she didn't want to go to school at this stage of life. School was for children, whereas she believed that practical experience would serve her far better in such a pursuit of excellence.

So, every day, Asma would hasten to complete her allotted *shalwars* and spend the remaining time until the shop closed observing Aisha at work. It was a sight to behold, Aisha bent over her sewing machine creating sleek forms of art that were the demand of every rich and fashion-conscious lady who entered the shop. These ladies, with their perfumed bodies clad in bright, starched cottons in the daytime and silky chiffons in the evenings, were the lifeblood of Akbar Tailoring. Their loyalty allowed Akbar to expand from a one-man operation ten years ago to this four-person shop bustling with activity. He fussed over their arrivals, plied them with snacks and soft drinks, and didn't allow them to leave until completely satisfied. Rumor had it that he loved each of his lady customers more than his own wife and children. Asma wouldn't have been surprised if the rumor was true because she had never heard a single word about his family in the two years she had worked at the shop.

Akbar was not alone in his passionate business. An entire row of tailoring shops lined the street outside. The clothing craft in Pakistan was certainly booming, supporting a sprawling textile industry that provided the highest quality and variety of fabrics to a hungry clientele. Women from all walks of life wanted nothing more than to acquire the latest colors and designs, and rush them to their favorite tailor to create an outfit worthy of their neighbors' envy. They spent years finding the perfect tailor, one who knew the shapes and measurements of their bodies in exquisite detail and had the expertise to suggest designs and fabrics that would showcase them appropriately to the world. Everyone knew that once you found the perfect tailor you stayed with him, no matter what. Tailors also knew they needed to do everything in their power to please their loyal customers, to keep them coming back each time ravenous for more.

Mrs. Malik was Akbar's oldest, most loyal customer. She was the one who had discovered his struggling shop ten years ago on a side street near the city outskirts and given him the chance to prove his sewing skills. Delighted with the results, she had kept coming back to fulfill her insatiable desire for the newest designs and the softest fabrics. She was the one who had recommended him to all her equally wealthy friends and relatives looking for the perfect tailor, and, when the women numbered so many they couldn't squeeze into the tiny shop anymore, she was the one who loaned him the money to buy this much bigger one in Saddar. He was indebted to her in more ways than he could remember, and each of his employees knew this very well. When Mrs. Malik's order came in, they all rushed to sew it.

Knowing that the lady in question would be arriving in a short while today, Asma was even more flustered than usual. She had completed all the pants the day before, even tried her hand at a more elaborate style of *shalwar* for the first time. She hoped it would be up to par, or Mrs. Malik's hawkish eyes would surely notice. But the clothes weren't the reason for her sudden shortness of breath. It was the anticipation of seeing who would enter the shop at noon.

For Asma, the seemingly plain seamstress, had a delicious secret that she hugged close to her bony chest. Last week, Mrs. Malik's order of clothes had been delivered by her husband, Ahmad Malik, a wealthy man who, despite his station in life, knew better than to protest when his iron-fisted wife commanded him to run an errand on the other side of town. Ahmad had delivered his wife's clothes a few times before, but last week the stars had aligned in a way that Asma had been alone in the shop when he arrived. She couldn't remember where the others had gone, one to buy lace from the neighboring haberdasher, another to eat a hurried lunch at a nearby café, perhaps.

In any case, being alone in the shop with Ahmad had revived feelings she had forgotten could even exist. She was aware of each of the five minutes that Ahmad stayed in the shop last week with every fiber of her being. The weather was so mild that the sweat circles under her arms were practically nonexistent, the fan was working perfectly to blow wisps of hair away from her face, and most wonderfully, if looks could speak, it seemed to her that Ahmad's eyes had spoken volumes in those five minutes.

Asma was no stranger to men's looks. It seemed to her that every Pakistani male over the age of puberty habitually leered at all able-bodied females in the path of his eyesight. Some women called it a nuisance, others a scourge, but for Asma it felt like a compliment delivered daily. It was a beautifully wrapped gift each time she walked out on the streets during the height of her youth. Those were the days when men only looked, when nobody dared to approach a girl for anything else. Now things were different and even looks could be dangerous. In any event, at twenty eight, Asma hadn't been the target of those infamous leers for a very long time. She had never felt their absence until last week.

Last week, she had felt like a different person. Ahmad had certainly been ogling, focusing all the brilliance of his sparkling brown eyes on her person. The situation was almost unreal, especially since she knew he was married and probably much older than her, yet she was flattered by his attention. It made her feel desired after what seemed like eons of invisibility. Asma was by no means ugly, but neither was she what most people would consider beautiful. While poverty had ensured that she kept her figure slender, it also meant that her skin had lost the luster of youth more quickly than it should have and her eyes had gained a look of sadness that often marks the poor. To have a man as wealthy and good looking – even if his looks were a result of lotions and massages, rather than Allah's grace – gazing intently at her was a boon to Asma's spirit. As she counted the pieces of newly stitched clothing in the bag and wrote up a receipt for him, she couldn't help but sneak little looks of her own and offer tiny smiles to counter his steady gaze. Then he walked out the door with a final wolfish grin.

"What are you thinking about, child? It's almost noon. Are her things ready?" Asma was rudely shaken out of her reverie by Aisha's loudly insistent voice.

"Yes, yes, they are ready." Asma arranged the bags of clothes on the counter, then turned to look surreptitiously at the mirror behind her. Perfect, she thought. Her *dupatta* was placed neatly on her shoulders, her hair was tied behind her in a long braid, and her clothes looked clean. She was glad she hadn't acquired the habit of covering her head with her *dupatta* like her neighbor Sameena. It would have ruined her hair and made her feel out of place in the little tailoring shop where none of the employees or customers covered themselves. They were all too modern and irreligious, she supposed, for everybody knew that devout Muslim women covered their heads with the *dupatta* or *chador*. Asma felt sorry for those women. Their covered heads meant that no man, rich or poor, ever ogled at them, ever paid them any attention.

The door opened with a blast of warm air, and she turned expectantly around to face her admirer. Only, it was not him but his wife who stood there, her plump frame disguised by the billowing yellow lace gown she wore. Asma's heart sank. It wasn't until that moment that she realized how much a chance encounter had raised her expectations. Exactly what had she wanted, though? A flirtation? A few kind words? She felt inexplicably let down and annoyed with herself for such useless emotions; without knowing it she bit her lip and blinked her eyes furiously.

It took her a few moments to realize that Mrs. Malik's face, too, was reflecting a myriad of inexplicable emotions. As the exacting customer rifled through the bags she kept glancing furiously over at Asma. Normally, the workers in the shop were pesky mosquitoes to be ignored. Why would Mrs. Malik be looking at her like this? A sixth sense was whispering inside her head, telling her something was not right.

Finally Mrs. Malik snarled in her direction, "Why are you looking disappointed? Did you think my husband would be coming to pick up my things?"

"What?" Asma's horrified and guilt-ridden question was echoed in a much louder voice by Akbar standing next to her. "Mrs. Malik," he asked, puzzled. "I don't understand, what do you mean by that? Is everything correct in your order?"

Mrs. Malik rifled through the bag and pulled out a *shalwar*. "Who made this?" she demanded, already knowing the answer. "See how poorly it is sewn? The threads are hanging out, the stitching is all crooked. I cannot wear this!"

Akbar tried to placate her. "Don't worry Madam. I will fix it right now while you wait. It won't take more than a few minutes." But the lioness had been awakened and there was no calming her down.

"No! I know this useless excuse of a girl is responsible for it. I want you to get rid of her right now!" Her voice was low but so intense that Akbar got the message clearly: either Asma leaves or I'm finding a new tailor. It was the sound of a death knell for Akbar, and he couldn't afford to die just when he was realizing his dream of entering the middle class. He turned to Asma and said quietly, "You heard her, leave. This was your last chance and you blew it."

Asma was reeling inside. She couldn't breathe. She couldn't afford to lose her job. Not now, with Nabeel so ill and no husband to support her. But what choice did she have, what voice against the veto-power of wealth? Everyone in the shop was staring at her in varying degrees of anger, indifference, and pity. She had no choice but to gather her tattered pride around her and leave.

Feeling dazed and strangely exhausted, Asma stood for a few long minutes on the sidewalk, not knowing which way to turn. She saw Mrs. Malik leave the shop with a flounce, step into her BMW parked illegally on the street, and drive away. Asma thought she would look back, but she didn't. She didn't have to, her purpose had been achieved. Questions raced through Asma's mind as rapidly as her heart was beating. How did Mrs. Malik know about her husband? Did he tell her? Why would he do that? Didn't he realize or care what would be the consequence of such an innocent exchange of glances?

There were no answers, of course. The rich didn't have to answer to the poor. She felt a warm hand on her shoulder and whirled around. It was Aisha, the mother hen.

"Asma, I'm so sorry. I should have warned you." She took Asma's hands, her elderly face lined with sympathy and worry. "Mr. Malik is quite well-known as a flirt, and he's gotten several girls around Saddar in trouble with his wife. You're not the first one to face that shrew's wrath. She's got her spies everywhere."

"But I'm innocent, I didn't do anything wrong," Asma was still in shock, and her protest failed to make an impression even on herself. "All we did was look at each other. Who would tell Mrs. Malik that?"

Aisha shook her head. "I don't know. Maybe it was Jamal. I never trusted him, you know. Anyway, what does it matter? What's done is done. Akbar isn't going to change his mind and risk offending Mrs. Malik."

"But what will I do now? My sewing isn't good enough to find another job. See what a mess I made of that *shalwar*? Who's going to hire me?" Her voice rising almost hysterically, Asma didn't know if she was asking Aisha or herself – or Allah. Surely someone would have some answers. She realized that despite the heat of the noon day, she was shaking.

"I have an idea. Remember the trade school I told you about? Where I studied to sew? I had told the principal you would come to see him. His name is General Kamaluddin, you should go visit him." She pressed a piece of paper in Asma's trembling hand. "This is the address; you go right now and see if he will give you admission. Once you learn how to sew well, you can get a good job like me."

Asma opened her mouth to protest, but Aisha slipped away with a wave. I don't want admission! Asma wanted to scream. I don't have time to learn, I just need a job so that I can keep my family alive! But no one was listening. No one cared.

As she walked shakily towards the bus stop, thoughts of her family – or what was left of it – swirled around in her mind. Her dear mother, may Allah grant her Paradise, had never been in good health, and Asma was born after four miscarriages. Neither her parents nor she herself had minded that she was an only child in a neighborhood filled with children. She grew up with lots of love, but her parents died within days of each other when she was just a teenager. The doctor said it was food poisoning, but, considering that he had no formal medical training, they could have died of anything.

And yet, what did it matter how they died? The end result was the same: Asma was left to fend for herself. A few weeks after their funeral she met her next door neighbor, Amjad, and they struck up a friendship based on the unsteady foundations of loneliness and boredom. In the absence of parents or other chaperones there was no need for decorum or modesty, but despite the freedom their romance was more a meeting of minds than anything else. It was he who proposed marriage, and, since she didn't have anyone else in the world, she accepted. He was a dedicated husband, she thought fondly, and life was good. Still, she kept waiting for the other shoe to drop. A year later, Nabeel was born. It was probably the happiest day of her miserable life.

Happiness wasn't hers to keep, though, and Amjad wasn't to be hers forever. She fingered the thin silver chain around her neck, the only gift he had ever given her and one she cherished. Perhaps now more than ever, because there was nothing else left of him to hold onto at night except Nabeel. Amjad had died in a horrific accident four years after their marriage as he was digging ditches for a utility company, a death that went unnoticed and unaccounted for among millions of others.

Even after so many years, it was a painful thing to recall. A coworker had lost control of his crane and swung the arm towards Amjad's head just as he emerged from his seventh ditch. In the span of a heartbeat she had lost her friend, confidante, supporter, and caretaker. What was a poor woman without her husband? She fumed anew at fate, at the injustice of the universe. The man in the crane had instantly disappeared. There was no inquiry into the accident. The utility company hadn't offered a single rupee to Asma as compensation, or even to pay for the funeral. She was left with her sad memories, a mountain of debts, a sickly son, and an old silver chain.

"Hey lady, look where you're going!" A passerby's snide call jerked her out of sour memories just in time to avoid the open sewer in her path. Damn those government officials who pocketed fat bundles of bribes but never sent anyone to close these open holes. One of these days someone is going to fall in and be seriously hurt.

She looked around dazedly, wondering where she was. With shock she realized that she had walked all the way to the other end of Saddar, past the noisy shops selling everything from second hand clothing to stinking fish, pirated music to freshly fried samosas. In front of her was an unassuming building with peeling yellow paint and a hand-painted sign announcing it to be "General Kamaluddin's Sewing School for Women". How had she found the way to this place when she was so lost in her own pain of past and present? She didn't want to enter, but thought her refusal might anger Allah, who had obviously led her here for a reason. She ignored the rumbling in her stomach warning her that she hadn't eaten anything at all that day and opened the door.

The school was quiet, almost peaceful. Asma could hear sewing machines humming in the distance, the quiet chatter of female voices. A servant asked for her name and then ushered her into a back room, commenting, "The principal is expecting you."

General Kamaluddin was short, balding, and dressed in suit and bowtie like the men she saw on Sameena's television set reading the news. He seemed to be in a grim mood, not unlike master tailor Akbar in demeanor. "So you want to study sewing?" he asked forcefully, looking her up and down and obviously finding her lacking. Why do all men who are mildly successful look so stern? she thought to herself. Does the sternness come later, or is it the reason for their success?

"Yes, I would like that," she replied bravely. "I can sew the basics, but I want to learn the elaborate designing, the latest fashions."

"Hmm, they all want that these days." He was silent for a minute, debating something in his mind. Then he asked quietly, "Do you have any money?"

Asma looked at him blankly. It was her turn to review his countenance and find him a tad stupid. If she had any money, why would she be here? She needed to learn sewing so she could get a job and earn money. Surely that wasn't difficult to understand. He was expecting an answer though, so she shook her head. No need to antagonize him needlessly.

The general handed her a pamphlet. He was obviously uncomfortable with the subject, but it had to be brought up. "This states our fees. As you can see we are not running an orphanage here. If you can find the money to pay one month's fees then I will give you time to pay back the rest of the months, on Aisha's recommendation. But you must pay at least the first month."

Her heart sinking, Asma didn't dare look at the pamphlet. What was the point? She smiled a mirthless smile at him. "Thank you for your time, sir. I will add this to my angel list." She turned to leave before he could comment on her cryptic response. Her exit was slow and dignified. She may be poor but her will was unbroken; she would find something else, *inshallah*.

As she emerged from the building, she saw that the shadows had lengthened and the cooler atmosphere had brought more people outside. The muezzin's call for late afternoon prayer echoed around her. Along with its soulful echoes she felt a curtain of despair descend on her, like a thick black fabric enveloping her from all sides and cutting off her breath. For all her bravado in front of the general, she was at her wits' ends. Everything is about money, she thought bitterly. What is one to do if there is no money? She walked sluggishly back the way she had come, wishing she could pray but knowing she would find no solace in empty ritual. The sky was harshly silent above her.

She walked back past Akbar's shop, and saw Jamal waving at her frantically. She wondered if he had, in fact, turned her in. What does he want now? she wondered. Are they going to accuse me of stealing something so that they can fire me one more time? She was amazed at herself at mustering the strength to joke about such a dire situation. Perhaps Akbar has changed his mind, she thought more seriously, pausing outside the shop. Jamal came running outside, his face full of worry. "Where have you been, Asma *baji*? Your neighbor Sameena called the shop looking for you. Nabeel has a very high fever and she's called the doctor."

Instantly and ominously, Asma felt a charge of electricity rush through her body. Not Nabeel! She started running, ignoring the calls from Jamal and the curious glances from people on the street. She saw a BMW driving slowly towards her and she barely registered Ahmad's face staring at her through the window. As she ran towards the street she fleetingly wondered if he was coming to see her or if he was going to ogle at some other girl in another shop. Her thoughts, a mixture of anger, frustration, worry and fear, gave her the force she needed to run to the bus stop, board the shabby bus that was, for once, right on time, sit through thirty agonizing minutes as it rumbled through clogged traffic, and finally thrust herself out onto her street.

Her feet seemed to have wings as she flew through the litter still lying on the corner, now burnt to a crisp and giving off the red glow of the sunset above. She found her house and crashed through the rickety door. Sameena was waiting inside the living room with the doctor, a real doctor this time, whose expression told her everything she needed to know.

"Nabeel is very sick, ma'am. His fever is extremely high, very dangerous for a little boy his age. You need to take him to a hospital as soon as possible, otherwise he may not survive."

"Hospital? Are you sure?" Could they hear her heart breaking, her wretched soul withering?

"Yes, I'm positive." He looked grave. It was easy to see that she couldn't afford the hospital. She swayed on her feet, then regained her pride and looked at him squarely. Like the general, like Akbar, like Mrs. Malik, he too would never know how wretched she felt, how scared and anxious she was. "Thank you, doctor. How much do I owe you?"

"Nothing. I was right next door, please don't worry about it." Seeing her utter lack of cognizance of anything except the news he had just delivered, he quietly left with Sameena. Asma sank down to the floor in a strange kind of exhaustion that left her limbs numb. The room felt hot and cold at the same time. Everything was eerily silent, as if even the pigeons and baby chicks in her backyard were numbed with pain. She looked around, noticing for the first time the stained walls of the room, the faded flower pattern on the low ceiling, the threadbare couch, the matching curtains she had sewed herself.

She squared her shoulders. She knew she should go into the bedroom to see her son – Allah knew he wasn't going to be with her long. But she couldn't face him yet. Couldn't meet the accusing eyes that silently asked why she couldn't save him. She had thought it would be a while before she would have to teach him about the unfairness of the world, about the vast chasms between the rich and the poor. But he was going to have to learn the lesson sooner and more painfully than either of them had expected.

All at once, Asma felt herself suffocating and rose unsteadily to her feet. She had to leave, if only for a little while. Maybe there was still time to find some work, a desperate solution to this agonizing dilemma she found herself in. She needed money, and she didn't care where she found it. But it sure as hell wasn't going to be found in her dreary living room where even the air was stale. She left the house and walked blindly down the street. She was beyond angry, she was tired of even her rage, because it had never given her anything.

Desolation and hunger joined together to make her deaf, dumb and blind. She left the neighborhood and entered the busier roads, scanning the heavens above as if in search of an angel's shimmering wings. Without a watch she had no way of knowing how long she walked. Cars drove silently by, windows rolled up so that the occupants could avoid meeting the tired gazes of those walking on foot. Ahead were bright lights, tall buildings, and that wealthy township called Defense, where Mrs. Malik and her host of perfumed and coiffured lady friends resided. She didn't know where she was going or why; it was getting dark and she should probably find her way back. But she didn't have the will to confront the inevitable tragedy that awaited her. As Nabeel's innocent face swam into her mind, she swayed, falling right into the path of a speeding car.

The car swerved, then came to a screeching halt beside her. Even in the dark, she could make out the huge shape; it was a Land Cruiser like the one preferred by several of Akbar's customers. Her dazed mind perversely wondered how much the car cost, as if intent on torturing her with thoughts of money she could never have, even if she sold her kidney ten times over. She heard a door open and seconds later felt, rather than saw, a form walk up to her. Asma couldn't care less who it was or what the person wanted. What could possibly go wrong now? Her world was already finished.

The form proved to be a woman, which gave Asma some measure of relief. At least she wasn't going to be raped on the side of a busy roadway. But what did this woman want from her? "Wake up, are you alright?" The woman shook Asma gingerly, forcing her to open her eyes. The scent of jasmine assailed her nostrils.

"I'm fine," she muttered, inhaling sharply. "I just fell."

The woman knelt beside her. "What do you mean? Why did you fall? I thought my driver accidently hit you."

"No he didn't. I'm just hungry. I fell from hunger." Asma couldn't bear another curious, pitying person staring at her. "Can you please go? I'll be fine, thanks for your concern."

The driver called out from the car, worry apparent in his voice. "Madam, let's go. She could be a thief pretending to be hurt in order to rob you. It's dark, please get back in the car."

Asma should have felt offended, but she knew the driver was right. She had heard reports of thieves pretending to be hurt on the roads, waiting to rob kind, unsuspecting souls who came to their help. The woman obviously agreed with the driver as well. She got on her feet and started to leave. Then she turned back and handed a small packet to Asma. "You can eat this. I hope you feel better," she said.

Asma looked down at her hand. It was a packet of wheat crackers, the type you could buy from any small corner store for a few rupees. These happened to be Nabeel's favorite, and he would often beg her for a bite. Nabeel! Had she actually forgotten him? The pain and anger came flooding back as she visualized her son's feverish face; it lent her a courage she didn't know she had. She grabbed the woman's sleeve as she walked towards the Land Cruiser. Maybe this woman who had stopped at the sight of a fallen body would help her where nobody else had.

"Madam, perhaps you can help me?"

The driver reacted before his mistress, opening the door and extending his leg out. "You! Stay away from her! I knew it was a trick!"

The woman motioned him to stop. "Wait, Hameed, let me listen to her. She seems like a nice girl." Nice girl? Asma realized the woman was old, much older than she had initially guessed in the dark. Now, as her eyes adjusted to the dark, she saw faint wrinkles in the corners of the other woman's eyes and mouth, a hint of sagging skin at the neck. Her dress was modest, just a plain embroidered white *shalwar kameez* that made Mrs. Malik's elaborate fashions seem gaudy by comparison. She turned to Asma. "Tell me what's wrong, *beti*."

No one driving such a fancy car had ever called her *beti* before. Maybe this woman was different, maybe there was hope after all. There was no way of knowing unless she tried. "My son is sick. He needs to go to the hospital, but I have no money. Nothing. Can you help me? Please?" It was a difficult thing to ask; the words stuck in her throat like yesterday's dry toast. Amjad had always said she was proud enough to be queen of a place called England. She wondered insanely at that moment, as she waited for the woman to respond, what England was like. It must be a paradise, the way Amjad had described it.

The driver was quick on the draw again. "See Madam, I told you! This is the oldest trick in the book. Her son is sick, indeed! You can tell she's lying, can't you?"

The woman smiled at him wryly. "You told me your son was sick just last week, Hameed. I gave you a lot of money for his operation, if I recall. Was that a trick, as well? Were you lying, too? No? Then let her speak."

Asma was amazed at the strength of the woman's voice, and a little delirious that someone was finally listening to her. Finally. "Thank you Madam. I am a hard working person, you know. I'm not a thief or a liar. I used to work as a seamstress in Saddar, but today I was fired by my boss. And my son is very sick; really, really sick. I'm not lying, I promise. I'll do anything. Please. Just help me!"

The woman was quiet for a long time, her brow furrowed in thought. Asma couldn't tell if her speech had been sufficiently convincing, and she waited with bated breath until the verdict was announced. Would her son live or die? Would she be saved by this angel or rejected by Allah Himself?

The woman made a movement towards the Land Rover. Asma sternly told herself that it was all right, that she would survive this latest disappointment. But she knew she was lying to herself. She closed her eyes slowly, only to fling them open with a rasping breath as she felt strange, cool hands on her own. The woman was handing her a package, she could feel a bundle of something – could it be money? – inside. She tried to stop herself from fainting. Was this real? What was the catch? Like Hameed, she didn't quite trust anyone or anything. How could she trust a rich person? How could a rich person trust her?

Yet her benefactor had obviously found it in her heart to trust her. Maybe the feeling could be mutual. Asma asked in a shaken, low voice, tremulously: "Thank you, but how can I pay you back?" It was a rhetorical question, of course, for her jobless, widowed status did not anticipate monetary success anytime soon.

The woman replied with another squeeze of her wrinkled hands. "Don't worry about that right now. I want you to go tend to your son. Take him to the hospital. Come back to my house in a few days, and I will give you some work. My maid resigned a few days ago and I'm looking for someone to cook and clean for me. Will you come back?"

"Yes I will, *inshallah*." They both ignored the incredulous cough from Hameed behind them. Trust, they knew, comes instinctively sometimes. The woman handed her a card with some writing on it; her address or phone number, perhaps. Asma took it slowly without reading; she was in shock and almost lifeless. Her only thought was Nabeel and how quickly she could get back to his side. The woman climbed back into her Land Rover and was carried away like royalty, leaving Asma and her package behind.

Like a starving man anticipating a feast despite his misgivings, she unwrapped the brown paper with shaking hands, ripping it in her haste. What if it was empty? What if it had all been a cruel joke? But no, this time her hope was realized. Inside was a treasure, or so it seemed to her naïve eyes. Rolls of rupees as thick as her thumb. There was enough cash to pay the hospital, she thought, marveling at such a miraculous display of prosperity. She turned the card in her hand and saw the woman's name printed at the top: Malaika. Her father had taught her rudimentary Arabic and she knew that name meant angel. *Alhamdolillah*! She hurriedly wrapped the money again in her *dupatta* and tucked it under one arm. It was time to go back home.

Amazingly, the journey back took half the time it normally would have. It seemed as if her feet, and her heart, had wings. She looked around her wonderingly as she half walked, half-ran, energized for no reason but a stranger's kindness. The almost-full moon was exceptionally bright tonight; she could hear crickets chirping noisily in the bushes on her left, even an occasional frog calling his mate. She yearned to be with her son, to prove to him that she could protect him, keep him safe. As she reached the boundary of her neighborhood, she started running at full speed, back towards Nabeel, back towards her pigeons and her chicks. She didn't need a watch to tell her she was late, but she knew that everything would be alright if she just ran fast enough. *Inshallah.*

Paradise Reinvented

The wind was strong tonight, blowing the dust in circles at Faisal's feet. He touched the letter in his pocket yet again as he waited under the ancient mulberry tree. The night was dark, the moon hiding behind dense, unmoving clouds that reflected his mood. The cemetery was always desolate this time of the night, regardless of weather. Superstition was rife even in the twenty-first century, Faisal mused, which is why this had always been their favorite meeting place. What better site to hide a budding romance than within the home of the dead? Only the macabre would suspect anything; not even the bravest would dare to follow them into the deep shadows among the crumbling graves.

She was late again. Faisal knew what that meant. Her punctuality was a sign of her commitment, he realized, because she had started arriving later and later in the last twelve months. Tonight he'd been waiting for more than forty minutes, toying with the letter until tiny paper cuts on his fingers silently screamed for him to stop. He already knew what it said – virtually the same words he had read in so many earlier letters. He didn't know why he had brought it with him tonight. Perhaps because he knew how the conversation with her would end, if she came at all?

The silence in the cemetery was oppressive, as if the inhabitants of the graves had much to say but their voices had been muted. He felt like a kindred spirit, more dead than alive, jailed in this earthen abode. He had never felt scared here, scoffing at the idea of ghosts and zombies that seemed to petrify everyone else. Death and burial was serious business, and graves were important tourist destinations in his hometown of Multan, the City of Saints. Any other cemetery would have been a hub of activity even at such a late hour, but this one held the bodies of no famous saints or important personages. As the final resting place of only poor farmers and laborers, it had been the ideal place to meet his beloved. Now, it might be the place where his love died a premature death.

He glanced at the gold plated watch on his wrist. He was young with all the pretensions of young men from upper middle class families – not seriously rich but with enough money to purchase the latest designer labels. He wore jeans and a t-shirt even though his father despised western dress, and refused to cut his hair despite the looks he received on the streets. His carefree style and ample spending money had won him many girlfriends over the years, but the one he was waiting for today would likely be his last. Wait a minute, where had that thought come from? He was reflecting upon this unexpected presentiment when he heard a slight sound behind him.

"I thought you would have left by now." She was finally here. He hadn't realized he'd been holding his breath until he let it out in a whoosh. She slowly walked towards the mulberry tree, towards him.

"Saima, you sound disappointed." It was more of a statement than a question. His hair, tied in a ponytail, defied its constraints within his worn baseball cap and struggled to be free in the strong wind. He wished his heart could do the same.

Her *dupatta*, slung causally over her right shoulder, was similarly flapping in the wind. She sighed, not meeting his eyes. "I almost didn't come tonight. There didn't seem to be any point." She paused, then asked hesitantly, "Any news?"

Faisal took the letter out of his pocket and offered it to her. She kept her hands at her side. He was amazed at how easy it was to judge her emotions from her body language. She didn't want to be here anymore. Not just at the cemetery, but with him. Her face was in the shadows, yet he could recall her beautiful features, her milky white skin and light brown hair cut in a fashionable bob, from memory. He was sure she was frowning in that delightful way of hers, although this time he knew she couldn't be cajoled into a better mood.

He unfolded the letter and recited the words he had already committed to memory. "Thank you for participating in our job interview and aptitude test. We regret to inform you that you are not a suitable candidate for our company. We wish you the best of luck in your job search."

Her countenance, or what he could make of it in the dark, was unyielding. *What a difference time makes,* he thought. With the first such letter, she had been defiant, hopeful; after a year of rejections, each letter had made her cry bitterly. Now she seemed drained of all other emotions, even the bitterness. She was almost serene tonight.

"How many letters like this have you received, Faisal?" she asked, obviously annoyed. "I've been waiting for you to find a job for three years now. It's useless. I can't wait anymore."

He felt compelled to ask, "What do you mean?" even though he already knew.

She squared her shoulders, as if about to deliver a huge blow. "I've received another marriage proposal. This time it's a doctor. He's planning to go to America for his residency. I would be stupid to refuse."

He understood. Marrying a doctor and going abroad was a dream come true for every Pakistani girl. It was a secure future, free from the perilous social and economic conditions they all lived in daily. A future he couldn't provide her or anyone else, not even himself at this point. After graduating from the prestigious Punjab University in Lahore with honors in Political Science he had come back to his hometown expecting rosy prospects ahead of him. His father was old-school, refusing to bribe anyone or use his extensive connections to find him employment. Fast forward three years of sending resumes, giving interviews, making phone calls, even knocking on doors, and here he was – a failure in the eyes of his friends, family, and especially the girl he loved. He was ready to take any job, with any kind of pay, but with millions of other educated youth willing to do the same, there just weren't enough jobs to go around. Not even close.

She left as quietly as she had arrived and silence descended upon him once more. After three years of love poems, secret glances across rooms, clandestine meetings among graves, he didn't even deserve a good-bye. He gazed around the cemetery with gritty eyes. The wind had picked up speed, howling with the same desolate intensity as his soul. He wanted to shed tears, but they were jammed hotly inside him after years of hearing that boys don't cry. As if boys didn't have feelings. As if boys were robots whose only job was to make others feel safe and provided for. As if they couldn't feel sadness, frustration or despair. He could easily have screamed or smashed the branches of the mulberry tree that had witnessed the painful scene. He was sure that would be considered acceptable male behavior. But Faisal felt it would be disrespectful to all the weary souls resting at his feet, so he refused once again to allow his swirling emotions to vent.

After a grueling hour battling his thoughts – wondering why everything bad always seemed to happen to him – he started back home on his motorcycle, a graduation present from his maternal uncle in Islamabad. The streets were dark and silent, for which he was thankful. He didn't need a thief or miscreant to test his limits and complicate matters even further. Nor did he need a police officer stopping him to ask questions. His pockets were empty and he couldn't afford to pay another hefty bribe.

The single-story bungalow where he had lived all his life except for his college days was in a well-kept neighborhood not too far away. At this hour, thanks to the devilish speed of his motorcycle, it took him less than ten minutes to reach it. He didn't want to go in, to face the emptiness waiting for him, but suddenly and inexplicably his bones felt so tired he longed for his bed. He let himself in quietly, a habit born of years of sneaking: first as a lad enjoying late nights with friends, and later as a young man craving a few stolen moments with Saima.

He thought he wouldn't be able to sleep, but he was dreaming before his head touched the pillow. Dreams filled with violence born of a strange, passionless misery. It felt as if only a few minutes had passed when the stern voice of his father roused him out of his fitful sleep. "Faisal! Come for breakfast!"

By the time he showered, dressed, and arrived at the breakfast table, his father was ready for a fight. "Don't you know what time it is, young man? I'm assuming you didn't wake up for morning prayers." The question was sardonic, and they both knew it. Not because Faisal wasn't religious – he was ambivalent more than anything – but because his father certainly wasn't a praying man. Faisal remained silent, the question a painful reminder of when his mother was alive. She would have asked him about his morning prayers, but in a very different tone. She had been extremely devout, not just the kind who prayed and fasted but the kind who cared for others, gave of herself constantly to all those around her. He missed her presence at the breakfast table sorely, not just today but every day for the last year since she had died.

The servant woman Halima brought out their breakfast – toasted honey bread, imported butter, piles of onion omelets and the ubiquitous Pakistani tea. He wasn't hungry, but he ate to pacify his father, wanting to delay the question he knew was on his lips. "I saw the letter from Sunrise Textiles in the mail yesterday. Did they respond to your job interview?"

He wanted to lie, but he knew his mother had abhorred liars. "Yes sir, they refused me the position." His voice was low.

His father's was not. "I don't believe it... again? What kind of a man are you, unable to find a job after so many years? Did you answer all their questions appropriately? Did you complete the aptitude test? You must have done something wrong!"

Faisal's hands shook as he buttered his toast. He refused to reply, to give his father the slightest indication of the flash of hatred the words aroused. He focused instead on his mother's memory, how he used to put his head in her lap and spill out his troubles. How she would kiss his face and tell him everything would be okay. Losing her was the real injustice in his young life, he thought with more than a hint of self-pity.

It seemed that she was on her father's mind as well, this morning. "Your mother was sure that her prayers would be answered," he said harshly, trying to provoke a response from his son. "I kept telling her there was no use in praying, but she was too foolish to listen to me."

Faisal stood up violently. "Don't you dare say anything about her!" he warned his father. "She was perfect. She loved me, she prayed for me, she knew I would succeed one day!"

His father laughed sarcastically, a rough, uncaring laugh that left him cold. "She died waiting for you to be successful. You disappointed her even in her last days!"

Faisal had heard enough. He leapt from the dining table and stumbled out of the room, making a beeline for the driveway. His father's loud voice followed him like a bad dream. "Don't think I'm going to continue to pay for your lifestyle, young man! I've already told my lawyers to cut off your spending money at the end of the month. I'm sick of enabling you!"

Tears streaming down his face, Faisal got on his motorbike and tore down the street. With no helmet and open wounds in his heart, he hoped he would crash and be obliterated. He rode at breakneck speeds down crooked town streets and big city roads, cursing himself at every killer swerve – wanting, needing an end to his suffering. What had he done to deserve this? Why had his mother died, leaving him defenseless against his father? Why had Saima left him too? The questions swirled in his brain, but he was too defeated and self-absorbed to find answers.

After two hours of blind steering, he found himself on a bridge over the Chenab River. He hadn't even realized he had come so far. What was he doing here? He wondered if it was fate, or God. He shook his head pitifully. In his case, it could very well be the devil instead.

The river was serene this time of the morning, a witness to ancient times. Faisal loved the peaceful waters. In fact, he loved everything about his Multan – an old city with a rich heritage of Sufism that attracted people from all over the world. Young, old, white, black, brown, they all came to view the tombs of the Sufi saints, take pictures of beautiful mosques, behold crumbling old forts with awe, and sample the delicious Multani dessert *sohan halwa*. Yet few people visited the Chenab River, despite the serenity and peaceful atmosphere. Nobody cares for peace anymore, Faisal thought morosely. They want to be out in the bazaars, eating, drinking, getting high, just enjoying the moment.

He didn't know when he parked his motorbike on the side of the road, or how he climbed up on the bridge rail, standing there for what seemed like hours. He didn't hear the infrequent horns behind him or the shouts of the curious few who passed nearby. For the most part, this stretch of road was deserted due to never-ending construction promised by politicians but never completed. He only felt the cool breeze in his hair, the stillness in his heart. He realized he was about to jump, but he didn't feel scared or anxious. He wasn't even angry anymore. He anticipated the look on his father's face when they showed him his lifeless body. Would he cry for his son? Would he be sorry for his behavior?

Faisal ignored the shouts getting closer behind him, took a deep breath, and felt himself falling. But something was wrong. In a second he felt that his fall was not outwards into the river, but backwards to the road, accompanied by a harsh tug. He realized angrily that someone had pulled him back from the edge. He didn't have time to turn around and look at his attacker; he struck the road with full force and blacked out mercifully.

When he came to, he was in unfamiliar surroundings. It was a dark room with unadorned prayer mats on the floor, shelves full of hardbound books lining the walls. He was lying on a makeshift bed in the corner, his head aching where it had met the road. He smelt food cooking, utensils clinking in plates outside. His stomach rumbled, giving him the energy to get up and open the door. Outside were several young men about his age, eating from a cloth on the floor like the one his servants at home ate from. They all had beards of varying lengths and wore *shalwar kameez* – the traditional Pakistani dress – in varying shades of white and cream. He marveled at them; he never missed a day of shaving, and only wore *shalwar kameez* on Fridays. How different they were from him. What was he doing in such a place?

One of the young men looked up and spied Faisal. "Oh you are awake, *Subhanallah!*" He had a chiseled face, dark brown hair combed back in a severe style, and a beard. He beckoned to Faisal, "Come and eat, brother, you must be starving."

Faisal realized that he was. He sat down on the floor with his new friend and took the plate that was offered. The *daal* made of yellow lentils, served with fluffy white rice, was a simple meal but infinitely delicious. He had seen his servants eat this when his mother was alive and he spent time with her in the kitchen. He hadn't known *daal* could be so flavorful, especially when eaten with bare hands in the traditional style instead of the fork and knife he was used to. Perhaps more importantly, he hadn't realized that in his present state of mind he could still feel hunger or appreciate the taste of hearty food. Despite his long sleep, his chest was knotted up with stress, his mind echoing with the hurtful words both Saima and his father had dealt him yesterday.

His new friend was speaking; Faisal forced himself to concentrate. "I'm Qadeer. I'm the one who rescued you from that bridge." Qadeer was looking expectant, eyebrows raised almost comically, as if gratitude was in order.

Faisal wasn't sure he was grateful, whether this Qadeer could be trusted. "I'm Faisal," he introduced himself with more than a little hostility evident in his tone. "What makes you think I needed, or even wanted, to be rescued from that bridge?" He thought Qadeer would be shocked, but the young man grinned in response. The smile was friendly but with an undertone Faisal found difficult to decipher.

Qadeer responded to his question. "I didn't know what was in your heart, brother. But when I saw you there on that bridge I thought that if this guy wants to give up his life, it should be for a cause."

Faisal was confused, forgetting his anger for a short while as he considered this statement. "What are you talking about? What cause?"

Qadeer's expression turned cryptic. "You'll see." He went back to his *daal*, motioning Faisal to do the same.

Between mouthfuls of *daal* and rice, Faisal looked around. In addition to the two of them, six other young men, similar in looks and hairstyle to Qadeer, were eating silently. There was no conversation; each was lost in his own thoughts, shoveling food into mouth with a distracted yet precise air. They kept their eyes lowered, ignoring Faisal and Qadeer as if the two didn't exist.

The room itself was large and airy, with a small open kitchen in the corner where a male servant was washing dishes. The windows were big, covered with simple grey curtains to keep out the sweltering Multan heat. Tonight, however, the evening was cool, and the curtains were drawn apart. He could see a narrow brick street lined with decrepit old buildings outside. With so many similar venues inside the old city, it was difficult to guess exactly where he was.

"Where am I? What is this place?"

"This is a *madrassah*. Names are not important." Qadeer paused, seemingly entangled in some mental exercise. "Or rather, names are very important, hence you should not know them."

Faisal wasn't sure if he was joking. "*Madrassah*? Do you mean one of those schools where people are indoctrinated with extremist ideologies? Or is this by some fluke an original Arabic *madrassah*, a source of infinite learning and education?"

Qadeer's eyes opened wide. "Ah, Faisal my brother, it seems that you are quite well-read." He smiled a huge smile that again made him look a little sinister. "Excellent, you will be an asset to the organization."

Faisal opened his mouth to ask the obvious question. But it seemed as if Qadeer was no longer in the mood for conversation. He stood up abruptly, wiping his hands with a cloth on the table. "Come, I want you to see something."

Despite the events of the past several hours, despite his self-hatred and self-pity, Faisal was intrigued. He followed Qadeer towards a back entrance, curious about what he would see. His motorbike was parked outside, waiting for its owner to reclaim it, and his heart skipped a beat. In this strange new place, the motorcycle seemed like a long-lost family member, but for some reason he hesitated to mount it. His uncertainty was well-founded. Qadeer strode up and mounted first as if he was its rightful owner. He pulled Faisal up behind him when the latter hesitated, and, with that simple action, their relationship was defined forever. Qadeer the leader, Faisal the follower. Qadeer the strong man, Faisal the petulant little boy. Qadeer the father, Faisal the son.

They rode silently for long minutes, until the traffic grew steady and clouds of fumes rose into their nostrils. When their journey finally ended, Faisal found himself in front of the tomb of the famous Sufi saint, Shah Rukn-e-Alam. Although he'd been here a few times as a high school student – the last time almost seven years ago when his mother had begged him to accompany her – Faisal tended to stay away from the many tombs and shrines in Multan because of his general unease with organized religion. Still, he was taken aback by the sheer beauty and majesty of this tomb this evening. The blue, azure and white glazed tiles and the immense dome on the octagonal building housed the remains of an eminent Sufi saint, making this not only a popular destination for hundreds of thousands of tourists, but also of extreme archaeological and historical importance. Gazing at this piece of history, Faisal felt his misery abating for a second.

Qadeer's voice intruded his contemplations and made him uneasy again for no reason he could pinpoint. "See the throngs of people worshiping this shrine?" Qadeer uttered with contempt. "This tomb and all the others in Multan are – *biddat* – innovations in our religion. All these people are not true Muslims. They are heretics who deserve to die."

Faisal opened his mouth to disagree, tension building up within him once again. He always felt annoyance when people spouted religious nonsense like this. He didn't mind devout

Muslims – his own mother had been an excellent example for him – but Qadeer's intensity and talk of violence was troubling him. He kept silent, waiting for the next revelation from his strange new friend.

"You don't have anything to say, brother?" Qadeer smiled a half-smile. "I thought for sure you would say something."

"Well, now that you mention it, your opinions are a little extreme," Faisal admitted reluctantly. His mind was itching, and he looked around for a way to escape Qadeer's stifling presence.

"I forgot, you must be thirsty after your meal." Qadeer took out a tiny flask from his pocket and held it towards Faisal. "Go ahead, it's nothing bad. You know I would never serve you alcohol, brother." He waved the flask slowly, "Drink!"

Faisal wondered if he had misheard the commanding tone. For a moment he contemplated refusing, but then the familiar anger took over and he felt a strange kind of heady defiance he hadn't experienced before. He couldn't trust Qadeer, but he really didn't care anymore. So what if it was alcohol? His mother wasn't watching him from Heaven, and surely he deserved to have a little fun. He grabbed the flask and drank, hearing the words "these people are heretics!" repeatedly as he gulped.

Faisal never found out what was in the flask. All he knew was that something powerful and mind-numbing took over his body that evening. He didn't remember much of the ride back to the *madrassah*, except that Qadeer asked him unending questions about his attempted suicide, his family and friends. Not once did it occur to Faisal to deny a response, or to lie. He may be irreligious, but his mother had raised an honest son.

The days passed in a blur, his body under some kind of tranquility spell that made him unclear and lethargic. He never realized that his hopelessness, despair and self-pity were growing exponentially each day, fueled by his own weak spirit and Qadeer's constant, somehow threatening presence. Unwilling to return home, Faisal remained at the *madrassa* to lick his open wounds, determined to forget his father, Saima, even perhaps his mother.

His only friend seemed to be Qadeer, who spent virtually every waking hour with him. He spoke continuously about Faisal's joblessness, calling him a failure and a loser in a paradoxically loving tone, reminding him that he didn't have anything to live for anymore. He probably should have protested, but he couldn't find the strength to argue. It was true anyway, the reason why he'd tried to end his miserable life on the bridge. Qadeer talked about his father, sometimes telling him that the man had died, at other times claiming that he was alive but didn't care enough to look for his son. Faisal wondered at this contradiction, but he firmly told himself he didn't care about the bastard who had thrown him out, whether he lived or died.

One day Qadeer told him he had gone to meet Saima, his beloved, and that he had found her to be a whore. Faisal should have been enraged, but he couldn't summon the effort. Why should he be concerned for her well-being anyway, when she had rejected him for some rich doctor? She deserved anything that she received at Qadeer's hands; only then would she repent of her cruel treatment towards him.

Qadeer's attacks were like well-aimed poisoned darts in Faisal's heart and mind. Already filled with a rage born of righteous self-pity, Faisal was like a ripe custard apple waiting to be picked and crushed. He began to transform into a fuming individual, hating the system that kept him unemployed, the women who refused to marry him, the fathers who confiscated their wealth. He didn't know it, but he was becoming more like Qadeer every day.

After four months of curses, threats, verbal abuse and the occasional drugs, Faisal was ready. In a secret ceremony late at night, he was officially initiated into the Young Multanis, a group of youth militants trained to carry out every murderous whim of their overlords. He learned too late that Qadeer was their city leader, whose duty was to recruit the most despondent young men he could identify and turn their hopelessness into fuel for human bombs. He was now one of them, for better or for worse. It was probably for the best that in a span of four months his pitying anger had been converted into full-blown, white-hot fury at everyone and everything he had ever known. The only person he refused to think about was his mother, blocking her from his mind completely and utterly. If she had truly loved him, she would never have died and left him to fend for himself. Whatever he became, it was going to be her fault. She would have to answer to that God she had loved so much.

Upon initiation, Qadeer relaxed his stronghold over Faisal in both physical and metaphorical terms. Another young man had wandered into the house they shared, and Qadeer had transferred his attention away from Faisal. Neither considered the possibility that, relieved of Qadeer's suffocating presence, Faisal might let go of his blinding rage just a little. Very slowly, as he learned how to use a gun and detonate a bomb, as his fledgling beard grew day by day and his ponytail became a thing of memory, Faisal started struggling silently against his emotional retardation. When he was ordered to kill stray cats and dogs as part of his training, he felt unable to express the robotic acquiescence he knew was expected, and barely hid the nausea in his stomach and the revulsion on his face as he complied reluctantly.

Too late, the actions of his father, even Saima, seemed more understandable as his rage left him drop by drop. Was he perhaps judging his family and friends too harshly? He couldn't be sure yet; in a way he liked being so angry because he didn't have to think, to care. Now everything was topsy turvey once again.

Yet his expression remained fixed and ruthless, mirrored in the faces he saw around him. The six other young men in the *madrassah* were perfect companions, making Faisal feel less alone even while refusing conversation and eye contact. Adnan was the oldest resident of the *madrassah*, unemployed for five years despite holding a master's degree in computer science. Haneef was the richest, the son of a company president who had lost millions of his father's wealth in gambling. Muhammad was the youngest, a recent high school graduate whose family had been killed in a car accident. Rehan, wrongfully convicted of his neighbor's rape and murder, had escaped from a mismanaged jail after serving three years of his sentence. Sarmad was a poor laborer, mourning the death of his wife and newborn son, while Rasheed had a degenerative disease of the brain with few symptoms and no cure.

Faisal found that he somehow fit right in the middle of this spectrum of desperation, self-pity and self-hate, although he was starting to wonder why he had given up on life after a mere three years searching for jobs. All the other willing prisoners seemed to have walked through hell to get here. The men shared a room, sleeping on mats on the upper story of the building, inches apart but each locked inside his own head. They ate together three times a day, studied religious books for hours, practiced shooting and even watched video messages once in a while from Qadeer's bearded superiors living safely in the mountains of northwestern Pakistan. Faisal called them all brothers, but none were his friends. There was no need for relationships or emotions here, not even for conversation.

One scorching Friday some six months after Faisal first arrived at the *madrassah*, Qadeer summoned them for a special sermon. Faisal was not one for congregational prayers, but he knew attendance was mandatory, as was everything else in this cursed place. Qadeer was especially ferocious that afternoon, spewing hateful tirades against any number of groups. Sufis, Shias, women, Jews, Christians – all those unlike Qadeer and his band of fanatics were fair game. Faisal's discomfort was palpable, but as he looked around he realized that it wasn't shared by his roommates. Words of hatred and promises of violence were infectious in a way that love and peace were not. They were headed towards some precipice, he felt intuitively, but what?

All was revealed after the sermon, when Qadeer handed each young man his suicide assignment on scraps of paper. Their missions were tied together, killing and being killed at different locations at the very same time. Multan was going to see a bloodbath like none other, and Qadeer seemed almost aroused at the thought, delirious with a bizarre conviction that transcended faith and belief. Despite the beard and the muttered prayers, despite the assurances that God would be happy at this purge of heretics, Faisal knew that what he was hearing was unlike any Islam he had ever known. Unlike the Islam his mother had taught him.

No one else seemed to share his doubts. Finally understanding the danger he was in, Faisal decided to keep silent for the time being and let God decide his fate. How ironic. Was he finally accepting Him, when it was too late for even the Almighty to intervene? The other men took buses to their assigned locations, but Qadeer insisting on accompanying Faisal, and the two drove together on the motorbike. Even though the mission had been secret, Faisal was somehow unsurprised when he reached his destination: the tomb of Shah Rukn-e-Alam. Qadeer left him on the shrine's external entrance and drove away to watch from a distance. Faisal was sure that any false move would be punished with a sniper bullet to the heart. Resigned to what would follow, he slowly walked towards the tomb, focusing his thoughts on the dynamite strapped inside his leather jacket. He felt numb, yet his anger was at the lowest point it had been for a long time. Without its crutch he felt suddenly bereft.

The shrine was full of visitors, men, women and children – the devout making a pilgrimage; the needy praying for intercession; shrewd businessmen selling everything from food to prayer beads. It was a Friday evening and the place looked different from his previous visits, perhaps because of his mood? Qadeer's hypnotic chants about these visitors reverberated in his thickened mind: "These people are heretics. The Sufi saints were not true Muslims. These tombs and shrines are all innovations in religion and they must be destroyed."

He repeated the hateful words several times as he stood there gazing at the hundreds of innocent humans breathing their last few breaths. He wondered about Allah, who he hardly ever thought about, but who so many others prayed to. Would Allah save these people from him? Would he really go to paradise if he detonated the bomb strapped to his body? His mother would surely be waiting for him in heaven, and she would no doubt be very disappointed. He was suddenly sure as he pictured her beloved, smiling face for the first time in months. Why had he locked her out of his heart for so long? Why was he thinking of her now? How could he face her if he killed these people?

How could he face Qadeer if he didn't?

Faisal stood frozen in the milieu for several long minutes. He slowly considered what his next step should be. In a sudden epiphany, he thought that perhaps praying at this sacred tomb might be helpful. After all, that was what the rest of humanity was here for. But how to pray, whom to pray to? Did he even deserve to be heard?

A vendor walked past, holding a tray laden with drinks of uncertain ingredients. He took a swig of a foul liquid which went straight through his body like an electric current. His mind, which had been struggling against self-loathing and depression for months, was suddenly startled awake. He felt as if all his senses were on fire, hyper sensitive and super sharp. Was it the drink or just his impending death? He could pick out individual voices from the babble around him – a young woman sobbing, begging for a baby; a man praying over and over for the health of his wife; an adolescent pleading for good grades. In a flash, he was more alert and attuned than he had been his entire life. He didn't know what he had just ingested, except that it helped him come to his senses in more ways than one.

He looked at the tomb and his mother's beautiful face came into view once again. He had visited this tomb with her, he recalled, and she had told him stories about the saint buried there – a kind, God-fearing man filled with light and love. To desecrate his final resting place with an act of mass murder would be against everything Faisal's mother had stood for, everything she had taught him. He looked around, hoping for a glimpse of Qadeer, but the recruiter was nowhere to be seen. Faisal was sure he was close by though, far enough to survive the bomb blast but close enough to make sure Faisal carried out his mission. He made a quick decision that felt welcome after months of numbness. If he was destined to die he was going to do it his way and he certainly wasn't going to hurt others in the process. How to accomplish that was the delicate part.

Feeling energized and free, he started running, dodging behind the flocks to avoid being spied by Qadeer. He needed transportation; luckily a plethora of vehicles were parked on the street outside the tomb, the owners too busy in their pilgrimage to notice if one was stolen. He found a nondescript Vespa bike and hotwired it awkwardly, recalling an *Everyday Mechanic* episode he had watched on cable television last year. Thankfully, his memory served him well and the bike started after just a few tries. He climbed on like a cowboy on his favorite horse, wondering how he had survived for so long without the trembling feel of an engine roaring underneath his body. He drove deftly, navigating people, animals and all manners of transportation – cars, trucks, busses, donkey carts, and so much more. He decided to stay within heavy traffic, acutely aware of the dynamite under his jacket and the detonation button in his pocket. The adrenaline was finally flowing, and so was he.

Not far from the tomb, he heard the roar of a familiar engine behind him: it was Qadeer, catching up to him on Faisal's own faster motorbike. "Faisal, come back!" He heard the words tearing towards him. "You're making a big mistake, come back before it's too late!"

Faisal hunched over and increased his speed, weaving in and out of traffic with impunity. The fresh air was a balm on his face and heart, erasing all his confusion and pain with each fervent gust. He had ridden faster than this many times before, but never with such passion, such thrill. He saw a police van and decided to stay close by. Surely Qadeer wouldn't dare open fire with police as witness? On the other hand, the police had a less than stellar reputation; there was no guarantee they could, or would protect him. Still, he knew he had no choice; he had to choose between Qadeer, the devil incarnate, behind him, and a sea of police ahead.

Imagining the sea gave him an idea. He changed direction, taking a ramp onto a major roadway. He finally had a goal in mind, because now he knew exactly where he needed to go. Funny it should have taken him three years of wandering to understand his purpose in life. In a few minutes, he was at the same deserted, unfinished section of the Chenab bridge, where his adventure had commenced many months ago. More and more, he was starting to believe in fate, maybe even in God, in Allah. He hurtled to a stop at the side of the road, disembarked quickly and climbed atop the rail, waiting for his nemesis to catch up.

Qadeer was seconds behind him. "Faisal, you're being so stupid! This is exactly where I found you!" He shouted, halting right behind. "Don't you realize that I saved you from death? Why are you doing this again?"

Faisal didn't turn around. "What you want me to do is death as well. Not just mine but the deaths of countless others. You call that saving me? You've just been using me for your own purposes."

Qadeer seemed earnest, a sincere madman. He put down the gun he was aiming at Faisal and tried to explain. "By detonating the bomb at the shrine you won't really be dying. You'll be going to Paradise as a martyr. That's living forever, my brother. Don't you remember my sermon today? We talked about this so many times. I thought you understood."

Faisal kept Qadeer talking to distract from the movement of his hand creeping slowly into his pocket for the detonator. "And all those people I will kill? Will they be martyrs too?"

Qadeer laughed mirthlessly, a chilling sound that echoed the seagulls above their heads. "They are heretics; they will receive their punishment in Hell. Don't worry about them. Just come down from there and back to the tomb. It's not too late. I'll forgive you if you just come back and finish the job."

"Is that all you care about, the job?" Faisal wanted to keep him talking, but more importantly, he wanted to understand why Qadeer and all the others walked this self-destructive path. "You think I can't see the self-hatred in your eyes, the misery and condemnation you reserve just for yourself? You exploited those feelings in all of us, but you, too, look at yourself in exactly the same way."

"Shut up! You don't know anything about me!" Qadeer screamed, his voice no longer suave and controlled. Faisal had unexpectedly caught a glimpse behind the bravado, and realized in his heightened sense of awareness that Qadeer's evil was a façade.

While he had tried to understand the other brothers in the *madrassah* and their motivations to join the Young Multanis, he had never extended the same courtesy to their jailor. Perhaps it was the light, but Faisal thought he saw genuine pain in Qadeer's bearded face.

"You think I don't know you Qadeer? I need only to look at myself to know you. We're all the same – you, me, the rest of the brothers in the *madrassah*." Faisal's voice was gentle, almost caring. He was so close; to fail at this point would be unbearable. "Your family must be looking for you. They must be hurting inside to see what you have become. How would they feel if they knew how many innocent lives you have taken?"

As with every human being, feeling judged by family was the last straw for Qadeer. He flung his gun on the road and lunged towards Faisal, his face contorted with agony and self-aversion. "Shut up, shut up!" His shout was like the snarl of a wounded animal.

Was he ready to do this? Faisal took a deep, relaxing breath, telling his heart to slow down and cherish its last few beats. He brought his mother's lovely face, smiling with love and pride, in front of his eyes. He was ready. So, perhaps, was Qadeer, locked up in his own pain and fury. "Shut up!" he kept shouting repeatedly, seemingly unaware of his surroundings.

"As you wish, brother," Faisal looked at Qadeer with gentle empathy. He closed aching, wet eyes and pressed the button in his pocket. Before oblivion – or was it after? – he thought he heard his mother's voice singing a lullaby in his ear.

Bittersweet Mangoes

It *was only eight o'clock in the morning,* but the promise of another hot day already hung in the air. Rabia Nawab, daughter of Malik Nawab, granddaughter of Peer Nawab, walked across the university parking lot, reveling in the sun shining on her perfectly oval face and the slight breeze caressing her wavy black hair. She spied a group of birds flying high overhead in a perfect V. They too, seemed to be enjoying the wind and the freedom to come and go as they pleased.

While many others she knew dreaded the arrival of summer, Rabia herself welcomed the delicious heat, but not because she had been born "contrary to everything normal" as her father had often said affectionately. Summer to her signaled regular classes at the university coming to their end, reading for pleasure, day trips, and most of all mangoes, the nation's favorite fruit. While summer back home in the province of Punjab was feverishly hot most days, the same season in her adopted city of Karachi, with its ocean breezes and milder weather, was refreshing and inviting.

As Rabia looked around at the other students crossing the parking lot with her, most bathed in sweat even at this early morning hour, she wondered if she was the only one who liked this time of year. Even her bodyguard Rehman, following discreetly in the distance, seemed uncomfortable. Perhaps it was enjoying the vast physical distance between herself and the rest of her family which made every season seem so much sweeter to her. She looked sideways at her reflection in one of the cars parked nearby. Her brightly patterned cotton top and neatly pressed khaki pants complemented her short, slim figure. She knew she looked good, no question about it. American fashions were all the rage among the rich young girls in Karachi these days, although she wore them with a unique style that was reminiscent of the actresses of yesteryear.

"Hey Gracie, wait up!" She didn't have to turn around to recognize the deep, laughing voice she had known since childhood. Six months ago, a local arts magazine had photographed her for their "Young and Restless" section, labeling her a Pakistani Grace Kelley. Despite her best efforts, the label had stuck, making her feel foolish even though she had not invited the attention. Today, she knew exactly who had the temerity to call her Gracie to her face.

Azeem caught up with her, sweating profusely. "You missed a great party last night!" He was unshaven and his eyes were red, but he looked as energetic as ever. "Why didn't you come? You might have enjoyed yourself."

They had reached the college entrance and she picked up speed. "Go away Azeem, find your friends. I'm not interested in your parties." Despite her words, she gave him a half-smile, her eyes glinting merrily. Azeem waved as he walked away, calling out, "Last day tomorrow! Woo hoo!"

Rabia shook her head resignedly as she waved back. Azeem was a family friend, and they had grown up as neighbors in their ancestral village in Punjab. Their fathers had both been active on the political scene until hers died four years ago of a heart attack, and his decided to retire from politics before stress won another victory. Despite the trappings of luxury that surrounded them from birth, neither Azeem nor Rabia had ever been particularly enamored of their respective fiefdoms, wishing for the longest time to escape beyond the control of their powerful families. She recalled the merry times of their childhood eating mangoes in his father's stables or running around her open farmyards. When Rabia left home to study in the International Business College in Karachi (or "the IBC" for short), Azeem, ever the loyal friend, had gladly followed. She was grateful for his presence. The years at IBC had been all the more memorable because of him.

A pointed cough sounded nearby. She looked up from her recollections, startled to discover a silent figure walking close to her. At six feet, Pasha was taller than the average Pakistani, with dark skin and an even darker expression. He shared some of her classes, but they had never spoken a word. She wondered uneasily what he wanted from her. For some reason she didn't fully understand, he always intimidated her with a strangely silent and angry look on his face. She told herself she wasn't scared of him, that he was just a fourth year business student like herself, but she felt butterflies in her stomach just the same as he directed the intensity of his gaze on her.

"Did you have to be so rude to him?" Pasha came straight to the point.

Her perfectly shaped brow furrowed. "To whom? Do you mean Azeem? He didn't mind, he knew I was only joking." She paused. "Well, half-joking. His parties are notorious for smoking and drinking, which I'm not really into."

It was Pasha's turn to look confused, but only slightly. "Drinking, as in alcohol?"

"Yes, alcohol." Rabia was amused at his naivety, happy that it made him more human. "You can get it from lots of places, you know. You just need to have the right connections."

"Which you both obviously have in abundance. Considering who you are." He turned to leave, disdain apparent on his face. But the short exchange had dissipated Rabia's fears and she inexplicably wanted to talk more.

"Wait, what do you mean, considering who I am?" She touched his arm to stop him from leaving.

"I thought that was self-explanatory." He didn't stop walking, and she had to take two steps to keep up with each one of his. She told herself that was the reason she was suddenly breathless, and not the sudden sidelong half-smile he bestowed upon her.

"What do you think I am? A girl, a student, ugly, pretty, what?" She was deliberately provoking him and he knew it. Rabia felt slightly amazed at her own audacity. Was she actually flirting with the unofficial ogre of IBC?

He didn't seem to sense the undercurrents in her tone. Or perhaps he was ignoring them, needing to make a point. "You are your father's daughter. Everyone knows who your family is. If we mortals ever forget it, your glowering bodyguard waiting outside your classes serves as a reminder."

"Rehman? Don't worry about him; he's just someone I have to tolerate. My brother insisted he accompany me everywhere." Rabia was talking too fast but she couldn't help herself. The thrill of finally talking to this tall, mysterious young man after four years of watching him out of the corner of her eye was too much. But he had also touched on a sensitive subject, and she wanted – needed – to set him straight. "Listen, I'm just a girl, trying to live a normal life. Have you ever seen me take advantage of my family's name or connections? I study as hard as anyone else here. I don't flaunt my money. What's your problem?"

Pasha seemed to lose interest, or perhaps he noticed Rehman closing in behind Rabia as if Pasha was an imminent threat to national security. "Nothing, I'm sorry I bothered you." With a quick movement, he turned and walked away.

Rabia spent the rest of the day focused on her conversation with Pasha. He was such a mystery to her, in fact to everybody at IBC. He didn't seem to have any friends, and he didn't really fit into the jet-set style of the other students. Although supposedly open to everyone, the exorbitant fees and stringent admission process of the college effectively restricted admissions, allowing mostly the wealthy to be ushered into its hallowed doorways. A few scholarships were available to give the impression of equality and accessibility and each year a handful of students stood out from the rest as the "poor kids".

Pasha was obviously one of these scholarship recipients. While the other students wore designer labels, his clothing was inexpensive and monochromatic. While the others sped around in the latest model Toyotas and Hondas – with Rabia the only one driving a Mercedes – he rode the public bus to and from the university, as far as she could tell. As she analyzed this she was surprised to realize how much she had been observing him for years without even knowing it. She didn't really care how much money he had – her experience with rich young men and women including those of her own family had been very disappointing so far – but she was infinitely interested in him.

Perhaps fate was on her side that day, or the universe was working for, rather than against, her. If she had been religious, she may have seen the hand of God. Whatever the reason, when classes ended for the day and she arrived at her aunt's house, her temporary home in Karachi, a servant informed her that she had received a gift. It was a basket full of big yellow mangoes, tied in a bow with a card that simply read the letter P.

Rabia's heart was filled with a strange euphoria. She intuitively knew that if confronted, Pasha would deny that he had sent the mangoes. In reality, except for the P, there was no proof that he did. But combined with that morning's exchange, all fingers pointed to him, which delighted her. How had he known that mangoes were her favorite fruit? Maybe he was just playing it safe; in the summer months, crates of mangoes were the gift of choice of all those able to afford them.

The mangoes fueled her curiosity even more. She wanted to know all about him – his life, his family, his past. Was the reason for his introverted manner a tragedy in his life? Did he have any friends outside the college? He seemed the antithesis of everything she had known in her twenty two years on earth, and she was eager to embrace this new knowledge.

At IBC the next day, Rabia sought out the one person who had graced her dreams the night before. He was stretched out on the ground in the commons area near the library, reading a book. It was the end of the day, and most students had gone home early to celebrate the start of the summer vacation. She sat beside him and said softly, "What're you reading?"

Pasha looked up, eyes narrowed when he realized who had found the courage to address him. He showed her the book silently: *Poverty, Growth and Institutions in Developing Asia.* That was interesting, she thought, an inkling into his thought process perhaps? Their professors preferred to assign a different kind of reading, usually related to American politics, culture or economics. Yet here was Pasha, reading about poverty in their own country. She had never met anyone who did that. She didn't want to seem too inquisitive, but her questions were growing by the second.

He seemed to sense her indecision; he also seemed more willing to talk today, for which she was grateful. "I found this book at the library. It talks about economic growth not being the only factor in reducing poverty. About how other kinds of organizations at the national and local levels can help with progress." As he explained, Pasha was almost staring at her, trying to gauge if her interest was purely superficial.

"Okay, that's good I suppose. But why are you reading it? As a business student shouldn't you be more concerned about making a corporation successful than reducing poverty? I mean, in a country like Pakistan, isn't that almost impossible?" She wondered if she had passed his test with what she considered pretty clever questions.

Pasha attempted a smile, but he could only produce a glimmer. "Though our professors would like us to think so, the truth is that business administration isn't only valuable for corporate entities. Look at yourself. With your background in politics and your family's fears about sending you anywhere without a bodyguard, you're probably not going to work at a bank or multinational corporation like P&G after graduation. But the concepts and practices you study here will be helpful to you as you one day manage or even grow your political party."

Rabia was intrigued. Managing her family's political empire had never appealed to her, but she let the unpalatable concept pass in her exhilaration that she was finally having an intellectual conversation with someone. The other students at the college spent more time discussing the latest celebrity gossip from Hollywood, than issues such as poverty. "What about you? How will you be translating this business knowledge? Something tells me you're not interested in a high-paying finance job."

His smile was more animated this time, as if a small door had been unlocked somewhere. "Actually, I have a small organization called Helping Hands. I started it several years ago and I feel that what I learn here will help me manage it better."

Rabia looked at him as if he had suddenly grown two horns. "Whoa! You are so ahead of all of us! What does your organization do?"

"We help families in the Malir Township. We do job skills training, give emergency assistance like food and water, and we encourage kids to go to school, even if it's just the local government school. *Alhamdolillah* volunteers from all walks of life give us hours of their time and expertise, including a couple of professors from the university." The small door was suddenly a floodgate of emotion which Rabia found irresistible. "It's hard work and, of course, we're not even making a dent in the overall situation in the city. But you can't sit still and do nothing when people need you. I've seen some positive results in the neighborhoods where we work, so I'm happy about that, at least."

Rabia was incredulous. "Pasha, that's awesome, really! Why haven't you shared this with anyone in the class before? I'm sure it would have made for great discussion and educated all of us. Maybe even the teachers."

"You think so?" Pasha remained unconvinced. "You think your friends care about anything except their own little lives? I haven't seen anyone show the slightest bit of interest in how the 'other half' lives."

"Well, I'm interested. This is why my father went into politics, to help the poor people of our nation."

"Oh yeah, is that the new party line?" Pasha was laughing at her now, and she knew it. She turned red.

"I'm serious! Nobody believes it, but *Abba Ji* was like that. That's why he and Azeem's dad, Uncle Sami, started the party in their youth. Don't accept everything they say in the news about us. Politics is a dirty game and both of those old coots knew how to play it, but I know that *Abba Ji* always tried to improve the lives of the people in our village. Maybe that's why he never got to be prime minister; you have to care only about your own ambitions if you want to reach the top."

It was apparent that Pasha didn't believe her, but he remained silent. After a pause he asked her, "Would you like to visit my organization?" It seemed as if he regretted the words as soon as they left his mouth.

"Definitely! I would be so honored!" Rabia stood up excitedly. "Can we go now?"

"Now?" The unease and regret on Pasha's face was visible. "I didn't mean right now. You're not dressed appropriately. You should be wearing at least a *dupatta.*"

"No time like the present." She caught hold of her hand and pulled him up. In her eagerness she didn't realize that she was touching him in a way many would consider improper. Yet even after the thought occurred, she didn't let go of his hand. It seemed so natural to be holding it, as if they were two pieces of a puzzle. "We can go in my car. I always keep a *dupatta* or two in the trunk in case I need to go shopping."

"In your car? You mean with Rehman? No thanks, he doesn't seem to like me very much." Pasha extracted his hand from her grip and gave a mocking salute to the bodyguard sitting discreetly a few feet away. "I'll give you the address and you can meet me there."

Rabia scoffed lightly. She wasn't used to acquiescing to another's will, even if that person was as handsome as Pasha. "Rehman won't care either way. Neither will my driver. They're not paid to have opinions. Come on, I don't want to get lost on my own. You know how hard it is to find the right address in this city."

Pasha reluctantly agreed. Trailed by Rehman, he accompanied Rabia to the parking lot, where her driver stood waiting by the Mercedes. "Salaam, *bibi,*" Shahid, the driver, offered respectfully.

Rabia was at once confident, in command. "Shahid, we are going to Malir. This gentlemen will tell you the way once we get there."

Shahid and Rehman exchanged looks but did not reply, since none was needed. Pasha and Rabia sat in the back together, while Rehman the stern statue deposited himself in the front passenger seat. As the gleaming car drove slowly out of the university grounds, hordes of students walking on foot moved out of the way like the parting of the Red Sea.

"So this is how rich people live," Pasha murmured, just loud enough for Rabia to hear. She raised her eyebrow in question, encouraging him to elaborate. "Think about it, how lovely it must be to drive around in an air conditioned car costing *lakhs* of rupees, when millions die from heat and starvation."

"Oh come on, Pasha. Don't preach to me. This is getting old. I'm not going to apologize for being rich!" She was getting a bit tired of his sanctimonious attitude and decided it was time to set him right. "I told you I want to see your organization, meet the people you help. What else do I need to do to prove to you I'm sincere?"

Pasha stared at her for a long time, as if unable or unwilling to answer her. Finally he spoke, and his eyes looked kinder and softer than before. "You're right. I'm sorry. Truce?"

She smiled, happy to have won the argument yet again. "Truce." In fact she was almost beaming. She couldn't wait to get to know him, and his world, better.

And that she did. In fact, the journey to Malir was a revelation in more ways than one. Rabia had never had occasion to visit this part of the city before, and she was amazed at the sights and sounds – and smells. The contrast with both her current home and her ancestral village in the Punjab was striking. When had the city erupted with color and noise? Perhaps the signs were always there, but she had never really opened her eyes and looked outside her tinted car window to truly see the humanity outside. She watched with amazement as colorful busses loaded with human beings clinging to all surfaces, including the rooftop, drove at breakneck speeds past their car. She looked on with horror as half naked children played in the streets with sticks and stones. She heard the powerful sounds of blaring horns interspersed with calls of fruit and vegetable vendors, lining the roads with their carts. She wrinkled her nose at the faint stench of open sewers, then marveled at the fact that she became used to the unfamiliar smell in just a few minutes. Is that how long it took to fall in love with a place, a person? She wasn't sure yet.

Pasha seemed to be enjoying the range of emotions on her face. He pointed out his favorite haunts: a *chaat* shop where he and his friends sometimes got together to eat and talk; the tiny mosque where he prayed on Fridays; the tandoor where he bought his *naan* from. She was fascinated, hanging on his every word as if it was a fairy tale and he the prince. She never saw the identically grim looks on the statuesque faces of Shahid the driver and Rehman the bodyguard. Even if she had seen them, she wouldn't have cared. After all, she was Rabia Nawab, mistress of them all, princess of her own little private kingdom.

When they finally reached their destination, it was almost evening. Yet the street outside Pasha's nonprofit organization, Helping Hands, was teeming with people of all shapes and sizes. The cacophony died down in an instant when the Mercedes rolled to a stop and Pasha and Rabia emerged from it. Pasha laughed. "See how you scared them?"

She realized that he was teasing. She nervously adjusted the *dupatta* on her shoulders, not used to wearing it for any length of time, and acutely aware of her khaki pants among the mix of *shalwar kameez* and *burqas*. She was anxious to meet these people, who had forgotten their initial awe and were crowded around Pasha as if he were a Muslim Santa Claus. The children pulled on his sleeve and asked for candy; the men extended their hands eagerly and insistently to shake his; the women stood around shyly but adoringly. Pasha was obviously the hero and Rabia was very much sidelined. Yet, for once in her life, she didn't mind in the least.

Pasha introduced her as a volunteer, which felt as welcome as water after a hot day. She smiled shyly as the circle expanded and she too was surrounded by adoring fans. "*Bibi*, you are so pretty!"

"*Bibi*, will you teach me to read?" "Madam, do you have any food, my children are hungry!" She was transfixed. Her hand crept unseen to her bag, as she prepared to shower the multitudes with more cash than they had ever seen before. Pasha grabbed her hand and shook his head emphatically. She instantly understood. They needed her, not her money.

"I'll come again tomorrow, I promise." She smiled brightly and happily. "I'll come every day, *Inshallah*."

• • •

This, then, was the beginning of a summer fling, a love affair of infinite proportions, and a lifelong dedication to a new way of life. Tomorrow led to the next day, then to the next, until an entire month passed. Before she knew it, two months had gone by in a blink of her eyes. Rabia became a permanent visitor in Pasha's dingy office, performing much-needed administrative duties such as filing and cleaning, which he himself seemed to have no time or inclination for. She met countless men, women and children, worked all hours in the free clinic, taught English at the free preschool and even rode the free food delivery truck. She was having the time of her life, so far removed from the realities of her family politics that it seemed as if Punjab was farther away than Mars.

She was finally alive, not only going through the motions, but actually living. She felt as if she was breathing pure, energizing life. The source of this heady power was Malir and its people, who seemed to have cast a spell on her in the span of two short months. Of all those encounters, some stood out as memorable in one way or the other. A few weeks into her volunteer work, she met a group of twelve year old boys who had just started training to be mechanics. She learned that two of them had been petty thieves and their friends had pressured them to join the class in an effort to steer them away from a life of crime. "Why do you steal?" she sternly asked one of the boys, disgusted at his behavior.

"Wouldn't you steal if you hadn't eaten anything for almost a week?" he shot back, looking at her with distaste. "Oh, but how would you know? You've never been hungry for a day in your life, lady!"

She should have been furious, but something made her silent. His words echoed in her mind all day and into the night as she lay in her soft, king-sized bed covered in imported satin sheets. Was it true? Did she really act so entitled that other people could recognize it a mile away? She wondered what had she gotten herself into.

The boys weren't the only eye opener, of course. Another day she met Ansar, a forty eight year old man who personified kindness and joy. She was cleaning out the supply closet in the free clinic one morning when he shuffled in with a bent back and a rickety cane, both of which seemed out of place for someone his age. She learned why when she sat down next to him in the tiny waiting room to take a much needed break. He had cancer, but he was not complaining. "I'm grateful for the pain medicines I can get from this dispensary, my dear," he assured her. "I'm ready to meet my Lord, so don't you worry about me."

"Your family must be really sad," she offered, her heart breaking.

"What family? My wife died in childbirth twenty years ago, and I have been alone ever since." Yet his smile never wavered. Rabia hurriedly wiped away the tear that escaped to her cheek, annoyed at her overflowing emotions. She wished she had a magic wand to wave away this man's suffering, the suffering of every resident in this township. When Ansar left, she stayed on the bench, turning her thoughts to the people of her own village. They too, were no different from these Malir residents, but she had never known them even in passing. Faces and voices revolved around her mind, echoing like elusive memories.

Suddenly Rabia wished she could fly back instantly to Punjab, to her village. She would walk the small roadways, enter the mud homes, hug the women and children. She would ask them questions about their lives, try to solve their problems. She had a vision of her father doing the same, so many years ago. How could she have forgotten? She recalled now that she would accompany him to his weekly visits to the village homes, playing with the children as he talked with the adults. Then, and now, she wished to be just like her *Abba Ji*. After years of meandering, she had finally seemed to find her path back to him and his dreams of a better Pakistan.

Some weeks later, Rabia met a young woman named Mahrukh: a slight young girl of eighteen, about to give birth in two weeks. Her face showed signs of a hard life, but her smile lit up the clinic when she entered. Rabia felt an affinity with her that she hadn't felt with anyone before. They spent hours talking, Rabia asking questions about life in Malir, life as a young mother-to-be, life in general. Mahrukh, after she overcame her general shyness, wanted to know about the latest fashions, what it was like living in a big house with electricity and servants. Feeling the spotlight, Rabia experienced an inexplicable shame. She recalled her words to Pasha at the college: "why should I apologize for being rich?"

That day, in front of Mahrukh, she did feel like apologizing. This was the tipping point: Rabia was no longer an outsider. Despite her designer clothing and Americanized ways, she was one of them. These – the teenaged boys, Ansar, Mahrukh and countless others – were not just people who lived on the other side of a great divide, they were *her* people, the ones her family heritage demanded she serve and protect. She was a Nawab, from a long line of politically active and socially conscious Pakistanis. Since when did it take a young, middle-class man like Pasha to show her the way?

Pasha, however, seemed to have abandoned her. He was usually absent whenever she arrived; whether by coincidence or by choice, she couldn't really tell. She wanted desperately to get to know him better, to peek behind that tough exterior and find the tender heart she was positive existed. Like the mangoes she loved, he too was there for the picking, she was sure. But how to begin, and where?

She finally got her chance one Saturday morning when she came into the Helping Hands office early in the morning, alone and unannounced. She found him loading the truck with loads of clothing, ready to deliver them to families in the neighborhood. "Can I come too?" she asked impishly, knowing she was annoying him but also sure he wouldn't refuse.

He hesitated for a long minute, surveying her crisply ironed cotton *shalwar kameez* and *dupatta* that covered not only her shoulders but her wavy black hair as well. "Well, well, this is a big change from Gracie of IBC," he teased. "I didn't think you even knew how to wear that *dupatta* properly."

She refused to take offence. "Yes, I do know. I asked one of the maids at my aunt's house. She showed me." Then, more anxiously, "Why? Aren't I wearing it properly?"

His laugh was unexpected, open, inviting. "You are wearing it perfectly! Come, we are getting late. I have a lot of clothes to deliver and very little time."

He extended his hand, and she took it without thinking. Only when he asked, "Where's your shadow?" did she blush and drop it, remembering the last time they had briefly held hands. She told herself that her newfound sense of modesty was more for his sake than hers. She had learned in the last couple of months that he was a religious man; she had seen the threadbare prayer mat in his office, the decorated Quran with earmarked pages on his bookshelf. She knew he wouldn't be comfortable with a public display of affection, and somehow she realized that she wasn't either.

She thought it was time to change the subject, and remembered that he had asked her a question. "My shadow? I guess you mean Rehman. He's at home. He was sick, so I gave him the day off. Shahid has gone back to Punjab because his wife is expecting a baby anytime. But what does it matter? I'm perfectly capable of coming here by myself, you know."

"Really? If you say so." He was still laughing as he swung himself into the truck and started the engine. She scrambled up at the last minute as the truck roared to life and settled in the passenger seat. This truck had quickly become beloved to her: the rattling, the fumes, the torn seats, all served as a reminder of where she was and what she was doing at Helping Hands. A reminder of her own transformation, her coming of age.

The truck's owner was equally beloved, although she hadn't admitted that possibility to herself yet. "So tell me about yourself," she commanded once she had caught her breath. She may never get a chance like this again, and she wanted – needed – to pump him for information. She knew his organization inside out, it was time she knew him too.

Apparently Pasha felt the same way. "What do you want to know?"

"Anything, everything! Who are you? Where do you live? What's your family like?"

He made a mock serious face, as if facing a camera. "I'm Pasha Sarfaraz, I live right here in Malir, and my family's the same as any family."

"What, wait a minute! You live here in Malir? I didn't know that!" For some reason she was shocked. He didn't look like the clients he served. He looked different, successful.

He looked amused. "That's right. I grew up on these very streets, just like all these kids you see. My father died when I was five, and my mother raised me, my younger brother and sister by herself. She did everything... cleaned houses, swept the roads, cooked and sold food, everything." He stopped, lost in thought.

"Wow!" Rabia interjected. "Is she still alive? I'd like to meet her. She sounds like an amazing woman!"

Pasha looked incredulously her way. "You'd like to meet her? Since when do you think the ordinary people of Malir are amazing? What's wrong with you Ms. Nawab?"

"Nothing's wrong. I'm still the same person I used to be." She was feeling defensive and it showed.

"Yeah, right." He slowed to take a turn, then sped up again. She was hot and a little nervous sitting with him in such close quarters. She really must have changed if being near a man was wreaking such havoc with her senses. Or was it just this man?

"Anyway," she changed the subject quickly to take her mind off him. "Where is your family now? Are they still..."

"Poor?" he smirked, enjoying her discomfort. "You can say it, being poor isn't an infectious disease, you won't catch it if you say it."

"Shut up! You know what I mean!"

"Okay, okay. My brothers are both doing well, *mashallah,* working at good jobs in banks here in Karachi. My sister is a school teacher in Quetta, and my mother lives with her. We are all fine and no longer... poor. Does that answer your question?"

"I guess." She thought deeply for a minute. There could be a lesson in all this, a way forward for her village if she could just put her finger on it. "How did you do it, how did you change your life around?"

"I don't know what I did. I have a feeling it was more what I didn't do. We didn't have much but we had Allah. I mean, my mother is religious and that's the way she brought us up. So I never got into drugs or stealing or gangs. I saw how hard my mother worked and I didn't want to disappoint her." He paused. "What else? I prayed a lot. My prayer mat has been drenched with tears more times than I care to remember, or admit." He looked at her sideways. "I know you're not the praying kind but you should try it sometime."

She didn't say anything, accepting the reality of his faith because it made him the person he was. She motioned with a hand for him to continue.

"I studied a lot, was lucky enough to get admission in a good school, then college. It was okay. I think if you stay away from gangs you don't fare too badly even in this township." He shrugged like it was no big deal. But Rabia had spoken to enough clients at Helping Hands to know what that journey entailed.

She grew serious under his gaze. "Joking aside, Pasha, I think that's really great. I truly admire you for rising to the top, making something of yourself. I don't think I could have done the same if I had been in your place."

The glance they exchanged was silent, yet spoke volumes. She realized that she wasn't only attracted to him physically but also respected him as a human being. The acknowledgment was a powerful signal, another turning point.

She started a bit as he asked a question of his own. "What about you? The whole country knows your father, what he did and how he lived, but what about the rest of your family? What are they like?"

She smiled ruefully. "*Abba Ji* was a great man. He really cared about his people... my people. He entered politics only because he wanted to do something for the country. But he became disillusioned early on. I think that's what ultimately killed him, the stress of having the power to make changes, yet being powerless against a corrupt system that is almost unchangeable."

"Your people? Do you want to enter politics too? Perhaps win some elections yourself?"

Rabia was horrified. "*Ya Allah*, no! Politics in my family is like drugs. It either kills you or ruins your life. I have seen what it does to people, I never want to go down that path." She paused, searching for the right words. "Though my brother, Pervaiz, loves it all. He's the party chairman now after *Abba Ji*, and he will do whatever is necessary to restore the glory of the family name. But I don't like his methods. I feel like he's not in it for the country, only for himself. He wants to be the next prime minister, if he can."

"Really? So where is this Pervaiz now? Doesn't he worry about his sister running around without her bodyguard in the middle of Malir, where gunfire acts as a lullaby for babies?"

"I don't know where Pervaiz is." She dismissed her brother with a wave of her hand. "I haven't seen him in four years, since I left home to come to Karachi for studies. He doesn't care about me and we don't really see eye to eye."

"About politics?"

"About lots of things. Like the fact that I'm not content to be hidden away in our mansion in the village, or that I want to get an education and actually do something with my life." She snapped her fingers and grinned. "Oh, and he hates Karachi, calls it a center of commerce and corruption. As if he doesn't remember that *Abba Ji* helped build a lot of the financial district here." She knew she sounded a bit petulant, but talking about her brother always struck a raw nerve. He was older by twelve years and as tough as nails.

Pasha was asking another question, seeming genuinely interested in her responses. "Then how come he let you come here to study?"

"I don't know, I think he just wanted me out of his hair. My stepmother Mona helped a lot. She convinced him to let me come, arranged for my aunt to keep me at her place all this time so that I didn't have to stay at the university dorm. And of course, it helped that Azeem was also coming here. You know Azeem... he's the son of Uncle Sami, *Abba Ji's* friend and our next door neighbor at the village."

"Yes I know Azeem. I always thought there was something between the two of you." The comment was quietly delivered, unexpected in content and timing. But she understood what he was trying to say.

She smiled gently, her heart exultant. "No, there isn't anything between us. I promise."

There was a long pause, not at all uncomfortable, but Pasha broke it nonetheless. "Where is Azeem these days, anyway? Back in the village next to yours ruling over the field workers and laborers?"

She shook her head. "No, he's gone to vacation in Canada with his cousins. I saw his missed calls on my phone the other day, more than ten in one day. I've been too busy to call him back. He must be really bored over there."

"Are you sure it's nothing important?"

"Eh! Nothing is important to Azeem. He's the most carefree person in the world. We could start the third world war and he'd be happily drinking his wine and dancing the night away."

Pasha was silent at this reference to a lifestyle very different from his own. He was staring ahead with a concerned look on his face. Rabia began to tease him. "What's the matter, cat got your tongue?"

He slammed his foot on the breaks, and the truck squealed to a halt with a shudder and sputter that testified to its age. "What are you doing, Pasha?" Rabia was horrified. "I'm only joking. We rich kids don't party all that much. It's just a stereotype, you know!"

He ignored her words and asked tensely, instead: "Who is that?" She looked at where he was pointing, and her world began to collapse in slow motion like the engine of the truck she was sitting in. A black Mercedes had approached their truck from the right, and parked itself in front of them at an angle, cutting off their path.

Among the ramshackle houses that lined the broken street, the car looked even bigger than it was, and somehow menacing. She squinted as a tall and hefty figure emerged; the breath left her body as she recognized it. She hadn't seen her brother in four years but his expression was the same as ever. Hard. Callous. Angry. She slowly opened the door of the truck and climbed out, reeling with the shock of seeing him so unexpectedly.

"Pervaiz, what are you doing here? Is everything all right?"

"Does everything look all right? You are sitting in a dilapidated old truck without a bodyguard and you ask me what I am doing here? You have been coming here to this cursed mud hole called Malir for two months, mingling with the scum of society, and you're asking me if everything is all right?" He was bigger than she remembered, his moustache long and thin, framing a face no mother could love. His voice was low and menacing, which she knew was a bad sign. But she had attained courage along with maturity in the last few months, and she couldn't let his opinions go unanswered.

"Scum? Is that what you call the people you are supposed to be serving? Have you forgotten why *Abba Ji* went into politics?"

"*Abba Ji* was a fool," Pervaiz pronounced harshly. "It seems that you have taken after him."

"Then I'm glad that I have taken after him, Pervaiz. I have found my calling. I am doing nothing wrong by helping these people. I'm doing something good. Why can't you understand that?" Rabia was confused as to why her brother was so incensed. She wasn't asking him to join her. She knew that to do so would be futile. Why had he come here, she wondered? What harm was she doing anyone by volunteering at Helping Hands?

Pervaiz was pacing angrily on the road, looking distastefully around him as if he might contract a disease. He finally turned, his face stern and unmoving, ready to deliver his judgment. "You are to return with me to the village immediately. I have decided what to do with you."

"Are you crazy, Pervaiz?" She couldn't believe what she was hearing. "You can't force me to do anything. I'm an adult; I can do whatever I want."

Pervaiz smiled a chilling smile, and the image of a shark came impulsively to her mind. "You are so stupid, dear sister. Studying here in this sin city, Karachi, has led you to believe that you are free. I own you, do you understand? Your leash has been so long that you haven't realized its presence around your neck. But now I am pulling you home, where you belong."

Rabia realized with dawning horror that he was deadly serious. It seemed that while she was changing for the better these past few months, he had been transforming into a monster, undetected. Or perhaps he had always been this way but she had been too young, too sheltered, to see his true nature. She backed away from him, towards the truck, wondering why Pasha didn't start the engine and rush her out of here, away from the harsh reality unfurling around her.

An instant later she knew why. A man she vaguely recognized as one of her brother's henchman had silently emerged from the Mercedes and hauled Pasha out of his seat in the truck, with a strong grip around his neck and a gun trained on his forehead. Rabia felt a cold stillness descend upon her heart, making her want to shiver but afraid the movement would set the gun off. She spoke to her brother without turning around. "Don't be stupid, Pervaiz. Let him go. He's got nothing to do with this."

"This man? He's the reason you've lost your mind!" Pervaiz glared in Pasha's direction. "Look at what he has turned you into. You, the pride and joy of the Nawab family, hobnobbing with miserable street folk. God knows how much of your wealth you have squandered on these unworthy people. On this Mr. Pasha.

Well, no more. You are leaving with me and that's the end of the story."

She felt someone right behind her, and whirled around. Too late! It was Rehman, her bodyguard, whom she had considered her protector until that instant. She backed away as he advanced, grabbing her bodily and striding towards the Mercedes. She screamed, hoping her voice would reach someone, anyone. But the street was strangely deserted, as if a sixth sense had dispersed the people usually thronging its stretch.

Behind her Rabia heard a gunshot, and the sound filled her mind with indescribable emotion until she thought it would explode. Tears of horror and infinite sadness pricked her eyes, of regret and a sense of losing something she had not yet owned. She started kicking and squirming, wanting nothing else than to join Pasha on the street. Yet she knew it was useless. Rehman had been chosen for his strength and loyalty by Pervaiz himself, and she realized that death was not her fate, at least not that day. She dimly saw a cloth descend over her nose and mouth and, exhausted emotionally and physically, she quickly surrendered to its sickly sweet perfume.

* * *

When Rabia awoke, she was lying in a bed. The room looked vaguely familiar. There was a picture of *Abba Ji* on the wall and a princess music box on the dressing table. She focused on the music box, trying to clear her mind of cobwebs. Her father had brought it back from one of his trips to America in the nineties, when she had been a little girl. After a few minutes of groggy inspection she realized that she was in her room in the village, where she hadn't slept in four years. How did she get here from Karachi so quickly? She tried to concentrate. Images of a nauseating car ride flashed through her mind: Pervaiz driving at breakneck speeds; Rehman sitting at her side; the dreaded chloroform cloth making its appearance each time she struggled to wake up.

How strange life had suddenly become, upside down and inside out. Her brother had become a maniac, Rehman the respectfully silent bodyguard was her jailer, and her dear Pasha was dead. She felt the dizziness rise up in her again, and she squelched it firmly. No! She would not give in to this madness. Whatever had happened, it was over. She couldn't change anything in the past, but her future was still waiting to be enacted. For the sake of her own life she had to be courageous and in a clear frame of mind. No tears, no fear.

She arose shakily from the bed and crossed to the door. As she had suspected, it was locked. She rapped loudly on the solid mahogany surface that had been especially imported from South Africa to match the furniture in this house. She firmly inquired, "Hello! Is anybody there?"

She heard footsteps walking away from outside the door. Perhaps it was Rehman, going to get someone who would let her out, answer her questions. She waited, swaying slightly. After a few minutes the door opened and a middle-aged woman stepped in, eyes lowered, holding a covered tray in her hands. It was her maid, Sakina, who had lived in the mansion for as long as Rabia could remember.

"*Assalamo alaikum, beti.* I brought you some breakfast." The aromas emanating from the tray reminded Rabia of how weak and hungry she was. Hot *parathas*, chili pickles, potato and cauliflower curry – she practically grabbed the tray with a heartfelt thank you, lowered herself onto the couch near the fireplace and began devouring the hearty food.

Sakina turned to leave, but Rabia called her back. "Sakina, wait, come here!" The servant reluctantly returned to her spot in front of her mistress. She looked scared, then astonished as Rabia took her hand and gently pulled her down to sit on the couch next to her. "Do you know why my brother has brought me here? What's going on?"

Sakina shook her head slowly. "I don't know much, *beti*," she murmured, wrinkled hands worrying the strands of her *chador* incessantly. "Something big is afoot, I can tell. The general elections are next year, you know. Your brother seems to be preparing for them much earlier than the previous time and your Uncle Sami has been visiting almost daily."

Rabia was not convinced. "But why would he kidnap me like this and bring me here against my will? Why would he kill Pasha?" Her voice broke. Killing someone in broad daylight meant that Pervaiz was desperate, but about what?

Sakina interrupted her thoughts in an urgent tone. "Pasha is dead? Your brother killed him?"

Rabia frowned, confused. "How do you know Pasha?"

"My niece lives in Malir, just a mile away from where Helping Hands is located. She often goes to their free clinic for medicines for her children. She phoned me a month ago to tell me that you were working there. I couldn't believe it! None of the servants could believe it!" Sakina's face was more animated than Rabia had ever seen before. "*Beti*, is it true? You were helping the poor people?"

Rabia was saddened at this question. Was it so unusual for those in her position to help those like Sakina? Why had she never cared before? "Yes," she assured the older woman. "I met Pasha in college, and he showed me a very different world than the one I had been used to. I spent all summer at Helping Hands, and I hope that I helped many people in those neighborhoods."

Sakina looked at her with a mixture of fondness, gratitude and respect shining in her eyes. She pressed a kiss on Rabia's forehead, brushing the hair out of her eyes fondly. "*Beti*, I raised you like my own daughter after your mother died. I was happy watching you grow from a child to a teenager, and then blossom into a lady. But today, hearing you talk like this, I feel like you have finally grown up. I am so proud of you. Your father, the great Nawab *sahib*, would have been proud of you."

Rabia's heart swelled. She wanted to talk more to Sakina about the father she missed so dearly, but the door flung open and Pervaiz strode in. With a squeeze to Rabia's hand, Sakina silently picked up the tray of half-empty plates and rushed out of the room, praying audibly as she left. Rabia stood up, gathering the tattered fabric of her dignity about herself. She refused to show Pervaiz how scared she really was. He may be acting like a madman but he was still her brother. Perhaps he could still be reasoned with.

"Rabia, I'm glad you're awake." Pervaiz said forcefully, almost rudely.

"I demand to know why you have brought me here against my will, Pervaiz!" Her heart was beating loudly in her chest, the memories of everything that had occurred in Malir yesterday flooding her mind.

"Yes, I'm sorry about all that." Pervaiz didn't look in the least bit contrite at having committed kidnapping and murder. Something was up, but what? "I received reports that you were mixing with the common folk in that ghastly part of town, and I felt that I had to bring you to your senses."

"Reports?" Rabia was bewildered. Was she really having such a surreal conversation with this killer? Surely her volunteering at Helping Hands wasn't the real problem. There must be something else going on. Something to do with politics, she was sure. In her experience, everything dirty could ultimately be traced to politics.

"Rabia, you must understand. You are part of this great family and you have to behave in a certain manner befitting your status in life." Pervaiz was deceptively mild, obviously leading up to a big announcement. Rabia decided to hear him out since she seemed to be a prisoner in her own house.

"Just tell me what this is all about." She was equally soft spoken, yet knotted up with dread inside.

Pervaiz took a deep breath, and turned to look out the window. "You know that elections are coming up next year. I am hoping to take the party to the highest level this time, and win on a national scale."

"But you are too young, nobody will take you seriously. And you don't have the money to win an election on that scale. You'd have to bribe thousands, call in favors, give rewards to so many. We may be rich, but we're not kings."

Pervaiz turned around, and she saw that he was smiling a chilly smile. "Exactly, my dear sister. I don't have the money myself, but I know somebody who can help me if we pool resources."

"Do you mean me? Do you want the money *Abba Ji* left me when he died?" Rabia couldn't believe there was an easy solution to this nightmare. "Yes, yes! You can take everything, I don't want it. Just let me leave!"

Pervaiz threw his massive head back and laughed. "Oh, don't worry, sister. That goes without saying. You are here now and I will use your money whenever I need it. But, alas, even both our inheritances together aren't enough for the amount I'll need." He paused for effect, enjoying the cat and mouse game he was playing with his captive. "Do you know anyone else who has that kind of money? A neighbor, perhaps?"

Rabia's brow crinkled as a horrible thought occurred to her. "Uncle Sami? But he retired from politics after *Abba Ji* died. Are you planning on kidnapping him too?"

Pervaiz's amusement increased; he laughed again until his big belly shook and his long mustache quivered. Rabia had never heard such a sinister sound. She felt a deep sense of foreboding.

Pervaiz continued after a minute. "My dear sister, while you've been having fun and living with dirty scumbags in Karachi, I have been very busy indeed. Uncle Sami has become my best friend in the last year or so; almost like a father to me. He definitely understands me better than *Abba Ji* ever did. He understands how important it is for me to become prime minister. So we've come up with a brilliant plan. He has agreed to come out of retirement and help me."

"Just like that? Out of the goodness of his heart?" Rabia was skeptical. She knew Uncle Sami; he didn't do anything without an ulterior motive. Even retiring from politics had been more for self-preservation than anything else. As a minister in the provincial government in the nineties, he had swindled millions of rupees from the treasury and then beaten a hasty retreat when threatened with exposure.

"Oh no, my naïve sister, not just like that. He will give me his considerable resources only if we are a real family." Pervaiz paused as if that should ring a bell for Rabia. "Isn't that a brilliant idea? If he becomes part of the family he won't be able to reconsider his commitment and back out like he did with *Abba Ji.* Did you know that our father would have won the elections and become prime minister twenty years ago if Uncle Sami had supported him?"

"Pervaiz, you are not making a lick of sense! How can he become a part of the family?" Rabia was exhausted from the events of the last two days and the sense of foreboding was deepening within her. "Will you just explain what's going on, why you've brought me here?"

"Don't tell me you're that stupid!" Pervaiz lost his patience and raised his voice, the better to intimidate her with. "How do people become part of a family, you fool? By marriage, of course! Our initial plan was to marry you to Azeem, but he found out and ran away to Canada where I can't reach him. So we've decided to go with Plan B and marry you to Uncle Sami himself."

Rabia felt sick. That's why Azeem had called her so many times in Karachi, to warn her of his father's intentions. She had been too smitten with her new life at Helping Hands to pay heed to the countless missed calls on her mobile phone, to the machinations in process behind her back. Marrying Azeem would have been bad enough when she was still grieving for Pasha, but being tied to an old man like Uncle Sami, whose reputation of cruelty to the villagers in his care was well known throughout this area, was positively repulsive.

She backed away from her brother until she met the cold, hard wall behind her. "You're crazy! How can you do this? I will never agree to this marriage, Pervaiz! Never!" She screamed at him, tears running down her face.

Pervaiz moved forward with lightning speed and struck her on the head with surprising force. He had never hit her before, and, as she crumpled to the floor with the might of the blow, she wondered if he was taking lessons from Uncle Sami. She vaguely remembered several women drifting into their village over the years from the neighboring estates, beaten to a pulp by Uncle Sami or one of his henchmen. *Abba Ji's* reputation of kindness attracted everyone who needed help; after he died that legacy had seemed to die with him as well.

And now his son Pervaiz had become the opposite of everything she and her father stood for, Rabia thought faintly as he loomed over her still figure on the ground. Her refusal had incensed him and he was ready to beat her into submission. His heavy-booted feet kicked her stomach, chest and head as she tried to protect herself with her arms – once, twice, three times. The pain was excruciating, blood trickled from gashes in her head and face, and she finally succumbed to her injuries. As she drifted into unconsciousness, she saw her step-mother Mona enter the room and ask quietly, "Did she agree?" and her brother answered grimly. "Not yet, but she will."

Perhaps he was right. Time slowly crept by. Pervaiz came into Rabia's room each day for a week, commanding her to marry Uncle Sami and beating her mercilessly every time she refused. Her pride, independence and intelligence ebbed with each blow. Growing up in riches, loved by her father, and protected from all types of horrors and miseries, Rabia had never experienced such hatred and pain before. She recalled a woman who had sought help from Helping Hands two months ago, running from an abusive husband. Rabia had looked with disgust at the bruises on the woman's face, wondering how a man could do this to someone weaker than himself. Even living among the poorest of the poor in Malir, she had felt a sense of safety and reassurance in her own privileged existence, knowing she would go back to sleep in her comfortable bed each night, never imagining that the same pain could be inflicted upon her by a member of her family.

After six days of physical and emotional agony, Rabia was at a threshold. She no longer remembered why she was refusing. Pervaiz was much stronger than her and she envisioned no way out of this horrific situation except to agree to the marriage. She had no one to turn to. Azeem may have been able to help her, but he had chosen to hide overseas. She couldn't decide if that made him a coward or extremely smart. Thankfully, Uncle Sami was nowhere to be seen. He had not entered her room yet, although he could very well be somewhere inside the mansion waiting for news of her acquiescence.

Any hope Rabia may have had in Mona's assistance had also turned out to be false. Although Rabia had never been under any illusions that her stepmother loved her, she had not imagined the extent of the woman's hatred. Now, even in her haze, she often saw

Mona standing alongside Pervaiz as he delivered blows and kicks, complicit in his behavior.

Sakina was the only one who had not declared her loyalties yet. Rabia hoped that her long-time servant would come to her aid. On the seventh day, instead of a tray of food being shoved inside her door anonymously, Sakina herself arrived with dinner. She hastily explained that Pervaiz and his stepmother had gone to visit their Uncle Sami in the neighboring village to give him an update on the situation. No doubt drinking and dancing would ensue, keeping them busy long into the night.

Rabia was lying in her bed, sheets soaked with dried blood and the stench of urine thick in the air. She opened her bruised eyes and tried bravely to smile at Sakina through cracked lips. She raised her head weakly from her bed and motioned the servant forward. Sakina was obviously scared, knowing what Pervaiz would do to her if he found her talking to Rabia. But she was here, which meant she wanted to help.

Rabia said to her maid weakly, "Sakina, please get me out of here somehow. Please, I'm begging you."

Sakina kissed Rabia gently on the forehead, whispering prayers. After making sure the young girl was comfortable she said, "Wait *beti*, I'll be right back," and left the room quickly. She returned soon with a basket of food and her husband Mansoor, one of the three drivers in Pervaiz's employ. Rabia remembered that Mansoor had also been *Abba Ji's* personal driver, taking father and daughter on many fun-filled rides around the countryside when she had been younger. How ironic that my servants are more loyal and loving than my own family, she thought. Maybe that's why I had felt an affinity with the people of Malir. Despite the challenges life put before them, they were kind to everyone.

As Sakina packed some clothes and personal items, Mansoor gently lifted up Rabia's damaged body in his arms. Every movement pained her, but she urged him to hurry. They left the bedroom and walked cautiously into the dimly lit hallway, Sakina leading the way towards the kitchen and servant quarters. This part of the mansion was deserted; the servants had probably gone to bed early in the absence of the owners. Without being detected, the trio emerged outside where Rabia's father's car was waiting. Mansoor gently laid her in the back seat, and husband and wife quickly climbed in front. In a few minutes they were flying towards the main road that led out to the main highway, towards freedom. Sakina kept glancing back in great fear, relaxing slightly only when they were an hour away from the mansion.

Assured for the moment of her safety, Rabia gave in to the urge to sleep. The motion of the car was intoxicating, and her body was infinitely fatigued. She woke some time later, gazing sleepily at the dark shapes in the distance, making out trees, farm buildings, a mosque or two. This route was so familiar, but never before had she traveled this bumpy road so full of fear. She looked at the couple sitting silently in the front seats. Images flitted through her weary mind; Mansoor bringing her a plate of mangoes after dinner, Sakina braiding her hair before bedtime. These two were dearer to her than she had realized. And now they were taking the ultimate risk for her sake.

"Where are we going?" She asked faintly. She was feeling equal bouts of dread and exhilaration; perhaps she was delirious now that she was in charge of her own destiny once more.

"We're going to Lahore, where we can get a train for Quetta," replied Sakina, anxiety lacing her voice. "That's the farthest away from your brother we can think of. It's easy to get lost in Quetta. And I have family there."

"Yes, Quetta. Pasha's sister lives there." Rabia felt a surge of emotion at the thought of meeting her beloved's relatives. How much there would be to talk about, to share, to grieve over. Then slowly, Rabia came to her senses. What was she thinking, including this elderly couple in her private drama? "No, you both have done enough for me. I can't ask you to leave your livelihoods for my sake."

Mansoor interrupted, kindly but firmly. "*Beti*, how can we go back to the mansion now? Do you think Pervaiz will let us live after tonight? We're the only servants still loyal to your father, and he will know that we helped you escape. It is better that we all leave together."

"Besides, you are in no state to even walk by yourself." Sakina continued when her husband paused to concentrate on his driving. "You need someone to look after you, just like you looked after all those people in Malir. Mansoor and I will gladly serve you in the same manner we have done all our lives."

Rabia felt deep gratitude well up inside her. She was beginning to see how much this dear couple had always sacrificed for her; now it seemed that they were happily going to make the ultimate sacrifice. If Pervaiz caught them, he would kill them as quickly and mercilessly as he done Pasha. While she herself was of value to him, they were flies to be swatted away. She admired their strength of character a million times more than her own or her brother's.

She tried to express herself as best she could, her voice dim but her emotions robust: "I cannot tell you both how grateful I am; not just for today but for every day of my life. I probably owe more to both of you than I can imagine. But we have to be practical; how will we buy train tickets, live in Quetta...?"

Rabia's sentence trailed off unfinished as an idea occurred to her. She struggled to sit up despite her injuries. "Mansoor, when we get to Lahore, find a State Bank branch. It will be morning by the time we reach there, and I can withdraw the money from my personal account before Pervaiz gets his hands on it. I was supposed to use that money for my fees next semester. It's not much, but it will be sufficient until I get better and decide what to do next."

Mansoor looked over his shoulder, his eyes shining with pride and approval. "Yes *beti*, I know you will do fine, with the help of Allah. You are your father's daughter after all."

Rabia leaned back against the car seat and closed her eyes wearily. "I am not only his daughter, but yours and Sakina's as well. May Allah continue to protect all three of us. Now drive faster please, I can't wait to meet Pasha's mother." And, satisfied for the time being, she succumbed to a much-needed slumber.

Tonight's the Night

Javed Gul, singer, guitarist and rapper extraordinaire, was on fire. Pacing around in the cozy reception room with its dark leather furniture and ornate accessories, he could hear the commotion from the crowd in the arena outside. His exhilaration was beyond words, beyond description.

From the clapping and shouting of the audience, to the poignant tunes emanating from the traditional *rabab* and *tabla*, all sounds enflamed him with a voracious hunger that was almost a fire in his belly. This night seemed like a Technicolor dream, so long in coming true that he had almost forgotten he had ever dreamt it.

He stopped pacing for a minute, just enough to breathe in the heavenly cacophony from outside. He smiled shakily, wiping suddenly sweaty palms on the legs of his new jeans. *Why am I sweating? I am so ready for this!* How excited his fans seemed, to hear him sing and perform. How amazing to even have fans! When he considered how long he had worked, how many obstacles he had surmounted to be here today, he felt proud and humbled at the same time. It was an unbelievable journey marked with tragedy, and tonight was both culmination and beginning rolled into one.

He glanced at the digital clock sitting on the granite counter of the mini-kitchen. It was still early; he was not expected on stage until 10:00 pm, which meant at least 11:00 pm by Pakistani time. He had an hour to calm down, eat something, practice his lyrics (as if he could forget even one line) and talk to a local reporter. He should also probably get some rest before the biggest performance of his life.

He caught a glimpse of himself in the gold-edged mirror on the wall. His lanky frame, day-old stubble, and longish black hair curling around the collar were familiar yet alien. Perhaps it was the blue jeans purposely torn at the knees or the cream colored button down shirt, more American in style than he had ever worn before, that were making it difficult to recognize himself. *Is this really who I am? Pashtun, Pakistani, American, rap star?*

He was standing in the middle of the room soaking in his unfamiliar image when the door flung open and Harris strode in. The same age as Javed Gul, Harris was shorter, rounder and much more sociable. With arms open wide, smiling from ear to ear, Harris exclaimed loudly, "What do you think, buddy? Isn't this amazing?" It was a testament to their friendship that not a single drop of envy could be detected in his tone. "Nishtar Hall, man, I can't believe it! We did it! *We did it!*"

Javed Gul was amused at this unbridled excitement; he wondered for a minute if it was possible for his stout young friend to actually burst with elation. But joking aside, Javed Gul understood exactly how Harris was feeling at this moment. The same emotions were mirrored in his own heart. The last five years had definitely been a roller coaster ride, and reaching the final destination – Nishtar Hall – was an undeniable feat. *We make a great team, me and Harris.* As different as hip hop and classical music, his artistic talent and Harris's business acumen together made an unlikely but brilliant combination.

"Yeah, man. It's all a bit surreal to me, too." Javed Gul agreed in the low raspy voice that had made him famous. "Remember when we first met? How people told us not to start a band because of the Taliban? Could you have imagined that one day we'd be standing here, of all places?"

In truth, Nishtar Hall was more a cultural landmark than a music hall, more a beacon of liberalism and political activism than a stage. In his heart, Javed Gul wanted to be one of those brave souls hailing the arrival of a more enriching era – one where art, culture and literary endeavors could supersede and hopefully defeat hatred, bigotry and violence. He knew he had big shoes to fill, but he was never one to back down from a challenge.

"I couldn't have guessed this is where we'd end up, not in a million years!" Harris shook his head slowly, as if absorbing the impact of the memories evoked. The two had met in college and instantly struck a friendship despite the differences in their backgrounds: Javed Gul, on a rare scholarship that allowed him to study after high school, and Harris, uninterested in higher education but going through the motions on the behest of his businessman father. Music was a passion for both young men despite the lack of a decent music or art scene in the austere environment of Peshwar. Javed Gul remembered fondly those college days of informal jam sessions: hordes of students listening to music from a single CD player hooked up with stereos or strumming popular tunes on secondhand instruments. *Ah, the simple, happy acts of a lifetime ago.*

Javed Gul hadn't been the only undiscovered talent in that college group. There had been other aspiring musicians, but, with hostility towards music growing over the last decade, some left the city in search of open-minded pastures while others developed more financially viable interests. By the time of graduation, Javed Gul and Harris were the last two men standing. Now here they were, preparing to be richly rewarded in money and accolades for their perseverance.

"Hey, listen! There's some food in the fridge." Harris interrupted his thoughts and pulled him back to the present. "Make sure you eat something before going on stage. You don't want to faint in front of all those fans, do you?"

It was meant as a joke but Javed Gul knew his friend was right. "You are so full of practical advice, *yaar*! What would I do without you?"

"Well, I know eating isn't a priority for you, man, so I thought I'd remind you." Harris looked genuinely concerned for just a second. "I realize that you tend to forget about the petty needs of this earthly abode, especially when you are working on a new song."

Javed Gul nodded his head wryly. It was a good thing that Harris was responsible for the business side of his music career, he thought, for what was probably the millionth time since they had first met. *Otherwise, I would still be singing lonely tunes on a broken guitar in my room.*

A buzzing ringtone filled the reception room, and instantly Harris the friend transformed into Harris the manager. Pulling his mobile phone out of his jacket, he mouthed the word "reporter!" as he strode out of the room. When he left, it was as if a wave of energy dissipated.

Javed Gul was still in a pensive mood. Ignoring the chicken sandwiches and fruit salad laid out on the counter for now, he stretched out on the sleek black leather sofa, marveling at its luxurious feel. Growing up a poor Afghan refugee in the slum neighborhoods of Peshawar, he could never have imagined that a sofa could feel so soft and cool to the touch. He recalled how he used to sit cross-legged on the hard *charpai* in his hut to finish his homework in the light of the kerosene lantern. He could never forget the harsh winters, the ache in his belly where food should have been, the ragged clothing handed down from dozens of other children. Life had been tough then, he mulled, and if pressed he probably could not put his finger on any one challenge that stood out among the others.

Thankfully he didn't have the time to dig into his unhappy past. Another knock sounded on the door, pulling him out of his reminiscences. Harris was back, this time followed by two others. A pretty young woman in her twenties, shoulder-length hair flowing unrestricted, dressed in a pink sleeveless *kurti* atop a pair of white jeans; an older clean-shaven man dressed in brown trousers and a faux leather jacket, carrying a professional camera. They seemed oddly out of place. While Nishtar Hall was certainly not a venue frequented by the stereotypical bearded men and *burqa*-clad women of Peshawar, Javed Gul was still a little taken aback to see this duo. Surely they were not a local news team? There was quite a strict, albeit implicit, dress code in the city, unsaid in words but enforced with glares if nothing else.

Harris introduced their guests hurriedly. "Javed Gul, you remember we had agreed to one reporter before the show? This is Nazia Basheer and her photographer Rashid. Miss Nazia is a freelance reporter from Islamabad and she'll be supplying the story to all the major outlets including online. You be a good boy now! I have to go take care of some other issues outside." He turned to Nazia and wagged his finger at her. "You've got thirty minutes, miss. Make them count, okay?"

Nazia smiled warmly at Javed Gul as Harris left again. "It's so nice to finally meet you, Javed Gul! I've been waiting for this interview for a long time! You have gained quite a following in Peshawar...among the youth, that is!"

She chuckled slightly at her own joke, and Javed Gul understood the reference. It was no secret that Taliban sentiments were strong here, with all types of creative activities viewed with suspicion by the older generation. Thankfully, many of the youth were a different matter. Peshawar's strict religious traditions jostled for space with its vibrant underground cultural scene – art, music, drama, comedy, it all flourished secretly despite shut-downs and violence. While some sections of society eschewed creativity as somehow sacrilegious, the younger generation found ways to circumvent the rules and enjoy life amid the opposition. More than anything else, Javed Gul loved this dichotomy of the city, and was somehow made more alive because of it. Certainly he tried to incorporate many of these themes in his music.

He gestured to the sofa he had just vacated, and Nazia gracefully accepted the tacit invitation to sit down on one end. He walked over to the mini-fridge, got out a cold Pepsi and twisted the top open. He joined Nazia on the sofa, as far away from her as possible, distracted by her tan shoulders and perfumed hair. He shifted uneasily. She may be from the modern city of Islamabad, but he was a Peshawar lad born and bred, preferring a little distance between men and women.

Rashid the photographer hunched down in front of them at a discreet distance, adjusting his camera as he waited for the interview to begin. He was darker than the residents of Peshawar, with a faint scar running down one cheek. His gaze was inscrutable. Was the scowl on his face solely for Javed Gul's benefit, or was it a perpetual expression on the photographer's face?

Nazia took out a tape recorder from her voluminous shoulder bag and set it between them on the sofa. "Okay then! Let's get started. This will be a full-length story about you, what your life has been like, what obstacles you have faced in the Peshawar music industry. Think of it as a way for your fans to learn more about you and also for aspiring musicians to get some inspiration. So please give elaborate responses. We'll speak in English if you don't mind. Since the article will be in that language, I'd rather record in it too."

English? Has she forgotten where we are? "Um, okay, sounds good," Javed Gul's voice was even lower than usual, and less confident than he had hoped. He wasn't sure he would like revealing the secrets of his life or his stiff English accent for this strangely confident, inexplicably attractive girl. But Harris had decided that this interview would be good for his career, and he owed it to his buddy to overcome his reticence. He took a swig of his Pepsi and set the bottle down on the floor. "What do you want to know?"

She smiled again as if to encourage him, and Javed Gul looked down awkwardly, unused to such directness. *Was she even Muslim?* She was wearing a *dupatta*, albeit swung casually around her neck like those scarves he had seen on billboards, so maybe she was Muslim but not practicing. *Wait a minute, don't be a hypocrite!* Since when had he become so judgmental, he who was often accused of being un-Islamic because of his music or his jeans? He told himself firmly how she dressed was none of his business.

Nazia was asking a question. He forced his thoughts away from her face and hair, and towards her voice. She was saying: "What was your life like as a child? Where did you grow up?"

Startled that anyone would want to know what he had been like as a child, he looked up straight at her. "I was born here in Peshawar, grew up here." He slowed down, trying to collect his thoughts. "I know it may sound strange to some people, but I really love this city. My family is Afghani. My parents and grandparents fled Afghanistan in the early 1980's during the Soviet invasion along with thousands of others. They were pretty well-settled there, and of course they lost everything when they came here. It's not a new story; millions have gone through the same thing for decades."

"Did you live in a camp?" The query was sympathetic. Who hadn't seen the television reports on the squalid, overcrowded conditions of Peshawar's refugee camps, catering first to the Afghans and later to the citizens of Pakistan fleeing their homes in the north, while the government conducted military operations against the Taliban there? He remembered watching crying babies on a news story not long ago, the images invoking a strange sense of familiarity that he didn't want to analyze further.

He returned to the conversation. "No, thankfully my parents had relatives here, so they were able to stay in the outskirts of the city in a poor neighborhood, in those early days, instead of in a refugee camp. But life was still a huge struggle." Javed Gul paused to take another sip of cold Pepsi, then continued the tale. "By the time I was born, things were pretty rough. I remember my mother used to embroider shawls to sell in the local market. My father and grandfather used to sell fruit on little carts they made themselves. I started working when I was four, doing odd jobs in the neighborhood and then working at a distant uncle's electronics store."

"I didn't know you grew up so poor." Nazia looked horrified, as if poverty was a fearful condition to be commiserated. Yet it was not pity on her face, but concern and fascination.

Javed Gul shrugged dismissively. "I used to hate it at the time, especially when I had to work those odd jobs – sweeping, picking up people's trash. But now that I look back, it was probably a good experience for me. I learned some important things, like sacrifice and humility, and gained a lot of skills that helped me later in life."

Nazia was looking at him with an overawed expression, as if he had just revealed that he was a superhero. *I'm just an ordinary guy, lady. I'm not even sure I deserve to be sitting here today.* He felt suddenly irritated at this rehashing of his childhood; he wanted to move on to happier topics. "I guess it's true, that time in my life was difficult, but not exceptionally so. As I said, it's the same story for millions of other people, especially for Afghanis. There's nothing special about me."

She seemed to understand the less-than-subtle hint and nodded slightly. "Okay, let's move on. You speak English, so obviously you've gone to school. How did that happen if you were so poor?"

"Things got better over time. My father was highly educated, and when I was about ten or eleven he was able to find a modest teaching job in a local school. The first thing he did was put me in the school as well. He always felt very strongly about education and he literally worked himself to his grave to ensure that I had a better future."

A vision of his parents rose unbidden to his mind – his father's silky black hair falling across his forehead as he read a book in the afternoon sunlight, his mother's smiling eyes as she helped her young son with the buttons on his shirt. He had loved them so much, and missed them terribly every single day. *Would they be happy to see me tonight, even though I turned out to be a musician?* He decided that they would. They had always been proud of him, showered all their affection on him until their deaths a decade ago – his father dying of a heart attack and his mother from tuberculosis in the same year. Their loss had devastated him, but his music had provided a welcome sanctuary from his emotions.

"So you think education is really important for our youth, not only in Peshawar but across the country?" Her tone suggested that she had asked this question more than once. He struggled to come back to the present, letting the images of his parents dissolve reluctantly.

"Education... definitely! It's the single most important thing that will get our nation out of the mess it is in today." Finally, they were talking about something else. Javed Gul became animated as he spoke about a subject close to his father's heart, and Rashid took the opportunity for some classic shots with his camera. "People who don't send their kids to school because they are poor and they need their kids to work don't understand that they are just contributing to the problems. If we look at developed countries, we see that their governments as well as their citizens paid special attention to education, even made education mandatory, and that's how they succeeded."

Nazia's perfectly made-up eyes widened. "Wow! You've really given this some thought! So you're not just a singer?" He couldn't decide if she was teasing him, but her manner was gentle and he experienced another twinge of attraction when she smiled that engaging smile of hers. He stared at the Pepsi in front of his feet. *Is this how she behaves with all her interview subjects?* He forced his mind back to the discussion before he went any further down an emotional path of no return.

In any case, she was right. Education was indeed an important subject for him. "Yes, well, that's what you get when you're one of the few who reach college, I suppose. I was able to get a scholarship from one of the well-off Afghani business families, and I'm eternally grateful for that opportunity. Economics and international government were my favorite subjects. Music was always just a hobby, I suppose. Who can think of making music a career around here?"

"Speaking of music, how did you get started?"

Javed Gul's smile was rakish, yet his manner pensive and almost moody. *How does any young man get started in music?* "Music was my lifeline growing up. I would say that more than anything else, music is the food of the soul for anybody who's going through challenges in life. Think about it, songs are written about so many different, real-life situations – a love affair, someone leaving, someone dying, money problems, drug problems, even God. We need music."

"Even God? What do you mean by that?" Nazia paused, her brow crinkling in a wonderfully endearing way.

"Of course, even God." Javed Gul leaned forward, much closer to her than he had previously been. He was unaware of Rashid's dark expressions and the camera clicking furiously. "Think about it:

so much of traditional, as well as modern music, is about God and religion. Not just here in Pakistan, where we have the *naat* and the *qawwali*, but in the West too, where they have Christian music in a variety of formats. It's because all human beings find solace in music of some sort. That's the problem with Peshawar, perhaps with all of Pakistan. The people who think music is evil and against the teachings of Islam don't seem to realize that melody and rhyme and creative lyrics are all over the religious landscape – the poetry of the Sufi saints, even the Quran itself is poetic."

Nazia was quiet, perhaps caught off guard. Then she shook her head in disbelief, smiling slightly. "Are we really discussing religion before your big concert?"

Javed Gul smiled back, realizing belatedly how ridiculous he must sound to this pretty young reporter from Islamabad, who wore her hair naked and smiled into the eyes of strange men. *Maybe it's time to loosen up a little bit, take a risk.* "Do you believe in God, in religion?" he asked boldly, not realizing how much he wanted to know her answer.

Nazia seemed startled, more by the question itself than the fact that the tables had turned and he was interviewing her. "Yes, I believe in God, in Allah," she responded slowly, deep in thought. "I don't pray as much as I should, and of course you can see that I don't wear the *hijab* or anything like that. But I think I'm a good person, I try to help others. Isn't that what Islam is really all about?"

Javed Gul nodded, infinitely pleased with her words. They had more in common than he had thought at first glance. He took a big gulp of Pepsi and swilled it around in his mouth, feeling strangely comfortable with her besides him, oblivious to Rashid's looming presence.

"Are you religious?" she asked the question tentatively, seriously, looking down at her lap for once. "Off the record, of course. I won't print what you say."

Is she really asking me such a personal question? It was as if she too, was feeling something, needing to know him better. "I like to think of myself as cultural more than religious. I like a lot of our local traditions, I'm not what you would call a very modern or liberal man, even though I'm in the music business. I keep telling myself I should pray more, that I should fast in Ramadan, but it's hard. I'm getting better at it, but there's still room for lots of improvement. In any case, my faith isn't something I wear on my sleeve. I think sometimes that it's considered "uncool" to be too Muslim in Peshawar, as if you're aligning yourself with the Taliban somehow."

His Pepsi was finished, and with it his need for private conversation. He felt the sudden urge to move and got up abruptly to stride towards the mini-fridge for another bottle. "Let's change the subject. You wanted to know more about my singing career?"

"Yes please, that would be nice! Thank you for reminding me what my interview is supposed to be about!" They shared a look that was part merry, part serious, as if privy to a secret joke that carried a deep message within.

He felt a warm thrill inside his body, deep in his chest that had been encased in ice for longer than he cared to remember. He coughed to cover his confusion, and came back to sit beside her, ignoring the glowering Rashid in the corner. "Okay, so about my early days in this cutthroat business. I was singing and writing music from my late teens. Especially after my parents died, I needed some sort of refuge, I suppose."

"Refuge from what?" She looked fascinated. He hadn't noticed before that her eyes were a hazel color. *Did she maybe have some Pashtun heritage in her?* He chucked inwardly. His mother would have loved Nazia, he was sure. He could just imagine her wagging a slender finger and saying, "get a ring on that girl before she disappears, *beta*!"

He responded quickly to stem his thoughts from entering dangerous territory. "It's hard to explain. Afghanis don't really get any respect around here, for a number of reasons, unfortunately. People don't accept you in their social circles, they don't treat you like equals, and it's really frustrating, almost grueling. I remember that my parents worked hard just to get by, yet there were days we didn't get anything to eat at all. I know that's not true of Afghanis alone, but it is certainly the situation I went through, and it was just very tough for me as a kid."

Nazia nodded sympathetically. "I understand. I've had many interviewees tell me about their prior lives and how they found it difficult to survive. Tell me about Peshawar specifically. What is the most difficult thing about living here in this city?"

"I don't know. If I had to choose, I think the worst thing would be the lack of law and order here. Of course it's the same in other cities now, like Karachi, but the situation is more stressful here; I think this is because we are so far removed from the rest of the country, and so close to the northwestern mountains where the Taliban are in control. Can you imagine what the young people in this city go through every day? Not knowing if they have any future? Not knowing when there will be a bomb blast or if someone will hurt them?"

She leaned forward, almost touching him, and again he felt a thrill that was hard to ignore, both in his body and in his heart. "How did you cope?" she asked ever so softly, her breath fanning his cheek.

He shrugged, not only in answer to her question, but also to shake off the attraction he was feeling for her. "Everyone has to find a way to escape, at least in their minds. Some people smoke *hashish*, others drink. I had my music. It was a way for me to forget the obstacles in my life and give vent to my feelings."

Click click! Javed Gul turned towards the intruding sound. He had completely forgotten Rashid the photographer, who was aiming the camera on the two of them like a weapon. He again wondered about the man, trying to grasp an elusive thought before it slipped away. He couldn't put his finger on it, but there was something not right with Rashid, or the way Rashid was working. *Something is definitely up with this man.*

Like a breath of fresh air in a stale room, Nazia interrupted his stream of thought with another question. "Javed Gul, tell me what influenced you musically. What type of music do you like to listen to for inspiration?" She was hanging on his every word, and he wondered why he didn't feel unnerved by her attention. After all, he wasn't used to girls ogling him, even if it was strictly professional. Then he remembered he was something of a star now, and his fans would probably include women as well. Perhaps this was acceptable behavior among the rich and famous? He grimaced inwardly at his own foolishness for making what the English called 'a mountain out of a molehill'. Yet he could foresee an enigma unfolding in his life: was the conservative culture of Peshawar changing, or was he the one whose habits and principles were being transformed through music?

He decided to ignore her steady gaze and answer the question. He had an interview to finish, after all. "I think my influences have really been all over the board. I've never pegged myself as just one kind of singer. In the beginning, I really enjoyed listening to a variety of artists, both Pakistani and American, as I tried to find my own place in the music world. I listened to many American rappers like Biggie Smalls and J. Dilla, for instance – their lives and deaths were similar to the violent surroundings we live in here, you know. For me, they and others like them were heroes in more ways than one. I also like listening to the folk singers of Peshawar, and

Afghani music now and again, to remind myself of my roots and to keep me grounded."

"It seemed from something you said earlier that your music started out more as a hobby?"

"Yes, I suppose it did, although to me it was more of an emotional lifeline. Only when I was in college did I really decide to put more effort into it. There was a group of students who all hung out and played different instruments. That's how I met Harris."

"Did this group ever think of starting a band? You have a couple of good bands in Peshawar these days, which started out in a similar way."

"No, there was never any chemistry. It was more of an extra-curricular activity for us, studying in the same college, getting together to let off some steam after classes. There were all sorts of people coming and going, there was even a girl or two. We listened to music, some of us sang together. I think I was one of only two students who wrote music as well. Harris came to me one day and said he could help me get some gigs in town. I thought he was crazy, but he can be very persuasive. So finally I decided to try it out professionally, although studying was always more important for me."

"So Harris has been with you since the beginning?"

"Yes, in fact he gave me the push I needed to get started," Javed Gul warmed to the discussion; his loyal friend was always a welcome topic. "We were pals from literally the first day of college, and he was always around, listening to me sing and play on the guitar. I guess he decided I needed his help! He's from a pretty well-to-do background, and he has some good connections. My first gig was when his dad's business partner needed someone to perform at a new year's party. After that, someone else his parents knew were having a graduation fling for their daughter."

"No kidding, you started out as a party entertainer?" Nazia laughed delightedly, but he instantly recognized that she was enjoying his story, not being unkind. *I need to lighten up, not take myself so seriously all the time.*

"Yes, that's right!" he agreed in a self-deprecating tone. "I did start out as an entertainer, catering to the upper class who could circumvent Peshawar's strict norms and have parties in their secure homes, away from the public's eyes. Harris offered to handle the business side of things – booking gigs, talking with the media, taking care of my funds. He's really good at that, and I'm very grateful to have him at my side. In fact, he invested the money I needed to record my album, *Roses in Prison,* last year. We officially signed a contract the last semester of college, when I started getting some decent reviews on the local music websites and we knew that we had gained a following. The rest, as they say, is history."

"Or the future." He could tell from her shocked expression that she hadn't meant to say that. To him at least, it seemed to be a very forward thing to say, typical Islamabad style, but he liked it. He smiled at her graciously, holding her gaze for a long minute to tell her that he hadn't been offended.

Nazia smiled slowly then, her journalistic professionalism fading a little. Her face became animated and more informal, as if they were long-time friends. "I've actually listened to *Roses in Prison* several times – not for this interview, but even before that. The album has sold really well, and the reviews have been great, but to me it seems very serious. You talk about death, poverty, giving up everything, standing up to violence. Those are some pretty deep topics. I'd like to know why you write about such things. I mean, you're in your late twenties, surely you can write about love or happiness or something light? What's the inspiration behind your music?"

My inspiration? Javed Gul was silent for a long time, mentally debating what to say. Normally he would have preferred not to answer what was essentially a personal question, but there was something about this girl that made him want to share his innermost feelings with her. It was as if they were alone. As if that surly third wheel, Rashid, with his shiny black camera, had become invisible.

Not for the first time tonight, he sensed that he was different – more on edge but also looser in inhibitions, less formal, less traditionally Pashtun. Was he vulnerable because of the performance ahead, or just lightheaded with hunger and drunk with fame? Was he being distracted by naughty thoughts involving the girl on the sofa next to him?

After a few minutes, he spoke, looking down at his new shoes instead of at Nazia or the camera. He dared to ponder if perhaps his emotional turmoil was not because of his present situation, but due to his past. Maybe he was feeling slightly guilty about something that had happened a long time ago. He decided in a swift instant that this was the right time to unburden himself, to finally talk about Shamsi.

He sighed deeply. Nazia signaled to Rashid to take more pictures. "One of the guys in my college music group, or whatever you would call it, was this really cool guy named Shamsi Ahad. Today you see just me and Harris as a team, but originally it was the three of us. Shamsi was a much better singer than I was... he had the most amazing voice and he could write lyrics that would leave you speechless." Javed Gul paused as he struggled with his thoughts. He had not allowed himself to talk about Shamsi for two years. This interview was going to be either very therapeutic or mentally devastating.

Nazia waved her hand in the air excitedly, gesturing him to stop. "I seem to remember a Pushto singing sensation called Shamsi

Ahad a few years ago. But then he disappeared from the scene, no one ever knew what happened to him. He was your friend?"

Javed Gul nodded, not sharing her excitement, not trusting himself to speak. After a minute, he swallowed harshly and continued. *It's time to tell this story, finally.* "Two years ago, Shamsi was already a sensation among all the college students, and he had quite a fan base. This was the time when the Taliban were even stronger than they are now, if you recall. Nishtar Hall was shut down, and you couldn't even sell music CDs in the stores. Still, Shamsi was bold and unafraid, and he continued to sing and perform in public locations. I was more reluctant and only performed at people's homes where they could provide armed guards, but Shamsi didn't care about all that. He always used to say, 'my music can't be contained: it begs to be heard.' And he did get heard. He was pretty famous in an underground kind of way. He raised funds to record two albums, even a few videos."

"What happened to him?" Nazia had somehow slid sideways on the sofa, now much closer than he would have found comfortable or appropriate if he had only noticed. But he was lost in his memories, and she was a child listening to a bed-time story, her expression flickering between fear and anticipation.

"His videos were all over the internet and local social media sites. The kids who liked his music shared his videos on Facebook, someone even put them on You-Tube during one of those times that it wasn't banned here. Next thing you know, he started receiving death threats – phone calls, letters in the mail – telling him to stop singing. Harris and I begged him to take a break, go visit his uncle in Karachi, but he refused. He was like that, stupid and brave all together, you know what I mean?" Javed Gul looked up, his eyes wet. This was one topic on which he could never keep his composure.

"Did he get killed?" she asked gently. What a world they lived in when death was the only plausible conclusion to Shamsi's tale.

Javed Gul nodded, running his right palm over his face in a gesture that unknowingly signaled exhaustion. What other ending could there be to Shamsi's story? It wouldn't be the first time a performer was murdered for his art, in Peshawar or elsewhere, and it certainly wouldn't be the last. "He was driving his car with the window rolled down and he came to a traffic stop. I was in the car with him; we'd been coming back from lunch at one of those little *dhabbas* – the street cafés with the most amazing food, you know? I remember we were laughing at a joke he had just told me, something so silly that it was just hilarious.

"Then in a blink, everything changed. One minute we were friends enjoying each other's company, the next it was all over. A man drove up on a motorcycle beside him, but we didn't notice him at first. He was wearing a cloth wrapped over his face and he took out this small gun, like a revolver, and fired several times at Shamsi. It was so horrible; there was blood all over us both. I shouted till I was hoarse and people around us were looking at us. They just sat there in their cars and bikes, staring at us. Then the light turned green and they all drove away, the killer too."

Javed Gul didn't speak again, spent from recalling his dark memories of violence, hate and indifference. Why had he thought revealing his anxieties would be helpful? He felt even more burdened than before. Nazia seemed to understand his need for silence. She waited several minutes before asking, "What did you do?"

Javed Gul looked at her oddly, piercingly. *You are definitely special, girl. No one has ever asked about me in that whole bloody incident before.* "What could I have done? I was left alone with my dying friend, and I was too traumatized, frankly, to do anything much. I just held his head in my lap and whispered some prayers as he died. The ambulance didn't come, no police, nothing. Sometimes I think that I was as useless as the bystanders. I couldn't save his life, I couldn't do anything."

"It wasn't your fault." She said gently, laying a hand on his for comfort. It should have been an exciting moment for Javed Gul, but he was too haunted by his past to fret about the impropriety of her touch. He took a deep breath and tried to smile; he didn't doubt that it came out as a grimace. *How kind you are, trying to comfort a stranger over something that had so happened long ago. Compared to the religious folk around here who would kill in the name of Allah, you with your modernized clothing and flowing hair are a million times more Muslim.* In the silence that followed, as they looked into each other's eyes, the clicking of the camera was conspicuous in its absence, Rashid's statuesque figure silently observing the tableau.

Javed Gul nodded, continuing the conversation as if there had never been any break. He wanted to keep talking, to clear his mind and his conscience. "You're right, it wasn't my fault, but the attack affected me deeply, I think. I found that even when I tried, I couldn't write about lighthearted subjects. It was as if all I could think about were negative things. For the longest time I was filled with anger and hate. I was questioning everything about my world, and I started writing the heavy songs that ultimately went into my album. You could say that Shamsi's death was the deciding factor for me to become serious about my own career. A few months later when Harris suggested we should form a team, I agreed. I felt that Shamsi would have been proud."

"You don't fear for your own life? The same thing could happen to you." Nazia looked horrified at the idea of living under constant threat. She looked around the room, fiddling with her slip of a *dupatta*, as if suddenly conscious of how close to him she was sitting. Her hand was still on his; hastily she removed it.

With the pressure of her hand no longer warming him, Javed Gul seemed to wake up from a dream. He blinked rapidly as if just now becoming aware of where he was and what he had revealed to this girl. He needed some time with his freshly bleeding memories. "Do you have any other questions? I need to prepare for the concert now."

There was that gracious smile again. She said, "Yes, yes, I understand. I really appreciate that you made time for us today. Any last thoughts, any message for your fans?"

Javed Gul deliberated for a second. Speaking from the heart was easier for him in his native Pushto language than in English, and he wanted to get this right. He coughed slightly, then looked straight at Rashid's camera. "To my fans, I'd like to say thank you for supporting me. It's really tough these days not just for artists but also for music lovers themselves. I know they take a great risk in coming here to Nishtar Hall so soon after the recent violence in our city. Art is a budding discipline in Peshawar; young men and women are doing incredible things, but they are not getting publicity for it because our culture does not accept it. We have a vibrant music industry, with bands and solo artists playing soft Pushto rock, English rock music, Pushto rap, folk music, and so much more. I am just a small part of this big picture."

Javed Gul turned to look at Nazia. What he was about to say next may not be acceptable to her. "You know, of course, that I have my critics as well. Is it okay if I say something to them?"

"Go ahead," she said, her voice low.

His eyes were deep pools of intensity. "We are the youth of Peshawar. We love our traditions, no doubt about it, and we try to honor them as much as possible. But we are also a new generation, living in this global village. We want to get educated, and we want to learn not only the sciences, but the arts, as well. We love music, painting, and drama, because we believe that we have God-given talents, because these are ways we can appreciate God, appreciate His creation."

He took a deep breath, going from the abstract to the real, to himself. "I love what I'm doing, because I feel that I'm offering the hope of a new tomorrow to so many people living in Peshawar. If I die today I will feel as if I have left a mark on this little corner of the world, and I'll die happy."

Nazia appeared slightly embarrassed, as if she had caught him in a private moment. She cleared her throat and nodded to Rashid. "Thank you so much, Javed Gul. We'll leave you to rest up before your big performance."

She gathered her bag, shoved the tape recorder inside and stood up, anxious to leave yet wanting to stay. Javed Gul watched them solemnly as they left. Nazia looked back, which he had been half expecting. Rashid too, looked back with a hard expression; perhaps he hadn't approved of the singer's emotional outburst. *What the hell is the matter with that man?* For some reason Javed Gul felt disquieted at the photographer's stare, but he didn't have time to analyze the premonition further before the door opened and Harris rushed in, yet again. His dear friend was sure to lose a few pounds if he continued this coming and going!

"Hey, buddy, you're expected on stage pretty soon. Did you eat something?" All other ideas fled Javed Gul's mind as he realized that it was show-time.

"No, I didn't feel like it. I did drink a Pepsi, though." Javed Gul wasn't much of an eater, especially before a performance. Of course he had never performed in such an auspicious venue before. "How long before I go on stage?"

"The opening act is coming to an end. We should go now." Harris informed him, glancing at his Rolex as they both walked to the door. His exuberance was more pronounced than ever. "You won't believe it, *yaar*, we are at full capacity, with a long line outside waiting to get in. Be sure to take in the view when you walk onto that stage tonight. That's what success looks like!"

Javed Gul laughed forcibly at his friend's enthusiasm as they walked out together into the hallway connecting the reception room to the main stage. Whether it was nerves or hunger, Javed Gul was feeling decidedly unsettled by now. *Surely I'm not scared of singing?* It had to be something else. Was it because of that reporter girl, or Rashid's inscrutable glance as he was leaving? Or perhaps he felt saddened by the memories of Shamsi flooding into his brain now that the dam of silence had broken. He felt like he had said too much in the interview, although this was the first time he could remember feeling uncertain about his words or actions.

Before he could contemplate any further, they arrived backstage. A makeup artist quickly sprayed some gel on Javed Gul's hair and roughed up his shirt so that it looked crumpled. He hated these pretensions, but he supposed this was the price to pay for the success Harris had mentioned. All of a sudden a calm excitement descended upon him and he forgot his earlier worries. He was at Nishtar Hall, after all. *Pretty damn cool!*

The drumroll sounded, Harris mouthed "Go!" Javed Gul picked up his guitar from the corner, jogged onto the stage, and the crowd went wild. Again he felt the fire in his belly, the rush from the sight of adoring fans more heady than the strongest drug. He could hardly believe they were waving, screaming, blowing kisses at him! With a nod to the young men – boys almost – at keyboard and drums, he grabbed the microphone and made it his own.

"Hi everybody, thanks for being here!" He probably should have offered the traditional Islamic greeting, but he didn't think it would make sense in this context. His fans were a mixed bunch of liberals and seculars: he could see bottles of bootleg alcohol scattered around, young couples holding hands, lots of youth wearing the jeans and t-shirts frowned-upon by their elders.

Somehow 'hi' seemed more appropriate, even though he personally preferred *assalamo alaikum*.

As he looked closer, though, he realized that this wasn't the typical rich crowd at daddy's business party. As he looked around he could see some conservative faces as well – girls wearing headscarves, older men and women in traditional Afghani dress. *Are all these people really here just to see me perform?* He felt humbled by the variety of his fans and once again reminded himself to stay true to who he was, even if he was famous.

Javed Gul strummed his guitar slowly to get into the rhythm. His first song was a new English rock tune nobody had heard yet besides Harris. He knew that many in the audience would know English, and it had become an accepted practice on the local music scene to include at least a few English singles in any album. Some singers went as far as to record only English tracks. He hoped that the new song would make a good impression, that he would make a good impression. He closed his eyes slightly, bringing the images of his music sheets in his mind's eye and began hesitantly.

> *Midnight.*
> *It's so dark tonight,*
> *And I'm oh so scared.*
> *Scared that I can't find you, mind you,*
> *Where in the world could you be?*
> *Heaven is calling,*
> *I feel like I'm falling.*
> *Will you catch me before I hit the ground?*
> *Tonight may be the night I die,*
> *I don't wanna hear you cry,*
> *Will you be there for me when I turn around?*
> *Turn around, find me, find me.*
> *Help me live again, love again.*

I need you to be stronger than me, better than me.
I need you to carry me in my pain.
Tonight.
Tonight of all nights.
It's going to be dark tonight.

He stopped and took a shaky breath; he couldn't hear anything over the roar in his heart. It took a few seconds to comprehend that the roar was from the crowd, shouting approval at the top of their lungs. He spied Nazia in the front row among other members of the press; she was sitting quietly in her seat, a figure conspicuous by her stillness among the fans standing, dancing, screaming. Was it possible to fall for someone in a single meeting? The idea dissolved no sooner than it had arisen. The band behind him had started to play the next song. He dove in, enjoying the performance now as much as the audience. *This is my night, and I deserve to have fun.*

An hour sped quickly along. Javed Gul pulled out song after song from his being, like a magician pulling a rabbit out of a hat. Pushto folk tunes, which the audience loved, mixed in with a few rap compositions and some more English refrains, all of which were interspersed with screams of "Woo hoo!" and "I love you Javed Gul!" It was an exhilarating, spine-tingling hour, and when they finally stopped for a break, his throat was hoarse, his shirt was soaked with sweat and his guitar weighed a ton. He had never stood for so long in such heavy lighting before, and a niggling ache was starting to develop in the back of his eyes. He was grateful for the Pushto folk dancers that arrived on stage at that moment to take over.

He left the stage to go back to the reception room for a much-needed rest. The silence in the hall appeared strangely magnified after the noise of the main arena. He stood for a while with his back against the wall thinking about Shamsi, wondering if his friend was watching from heaven. *You didn't deserve to die, pal, but I hope I'm making you proud.* Despite his elation at singing in front of such a big, receptive crowd, the strange tension he'd been feeling earlier had now returned much stronger. His footsteps made echoing sounds that inexplicably seemed hollow and menacing. I should have listened to Harris and eaten something, he thought, trying to dispel his uneasiness. He heard a firecracker and then a faint scream that was different from the screams of his fans. What the hell was going on?

He strode towards his room; before he was halfway to it he saw the door swing open and Nazia rush out. The scene didn't make sense to him in a number of ways, and questions swirled around his adrenalin infused brain. Why was she coming out from his room? Why was she holding her arm like that? Why was she running? And then finally, did she come to give him her number, or to say something? That last thought seemed ridiculous, yet his heart was beating faster than it had been in front of his fans.

All expectations of a private meeting with Nazia evaporated as she reached him, panting heavily and looking more than a little scared. He realized that blood was flowing from her right arm. It finally struck him why she looked so different: her *dupatta* was missing. In Peshawar, girls did not just leave their *dupatta* behind, not even the most westernized ones. More than the blood, that missing piece of garment was what alerted him to the fact that something was very wrong. He held her hand tightly, forgetting all modesty, and asked urgently: "What happened?"

She was obviously shaken but trying to calm herself down. Taking deep breaths, she said, "I went back to your room because I remembered I had left some papers there. Rashid was hiding there in the dark. Javed, he's got a gun!"

"Rashid, your photographer?" He was confused but at the same time, something clicked into place in his mind. He knew what she was going to say before she said it.

"Yes, Rashid. He's not my regular guy. I found him online, he said he was freelance. I was desperate to do this interview so I didn't dig too deep. He said that he's connected with the Taliban, although I don't know if I believe it. But he is deranged, I'll tell you that. He was obviously waiting for you and I guess he didn't see me in the dark so he shot at me instead. Thank God he missed."

"Shit!" Javed tore off his shirt and wrapped it around her wounded arm. "I'm going to try to hold him off. You go get some help."

"Hold him off? What are you, James Bond?" He was impressed that she could jest with blood pouring down her arm.

She tried to tug him in the opposite direction. "Come outside with me. We need to get away from here, you idiot!"

Javed Gul shook his head. Those were his fans out there, and Harris, the closest thing to a family he had had in a long time. And suddenly he felt an urge to protect Nazia, to stake his claim. "No, I have to make sure he doesn't run out into the audience with a gun. Go get help."

"Who? The police aren't going to come, you know that!"

"I have a couple of security guys in the front. They've got guns. Go get them, quickly!" He pushed her in the opposite direction and then, squaring his naked shoulders, walked purposefully towards the reception room. He waited outside for several long minutes, gathering the courage to enter. He had told Nazia during the interview that he was not afraid to die, but he realized that it had been a lie. He wanted to live, make music, find out if a feisty reporter from Islamabad could be the perfect girl for him. But it seemed that the song he had sung on stage was coming true: *Tonight may be the night I die.* He took a mental double-take. Was he really singing his own song in his head as he prepared to meet his end? *How dumb, how arrogant! Wouldn't a prayer be more appropriate?*

No sense in delaying the inevitable. Before he turned the doorknob he looked back again to make sure Nazia was gone. The two security guards he had hired for the night were striding towards him, their huge mustaches just a tad smaller in size than their guns. Assured of their backup, he entered the darkened reception room, to be met almost immediately with the sound of a gunshot. In the confines of the reception room, the echo was much louder than a firecracker, and he was suddenly transported to another time two years ago when he had faced another killer with a gun.

Tonight, however, he didn't feel anger or fear. This was Rashid after all, the guy in a faux-leather jacket who had been taking his pictures a couple of hours ago. "What're you doing, buddy? Put that gun down before you hurt yourself." Ever the calm negotiator, Javed Gul thought he should at least try to reason with this madman.

"I heard what you said in the interview. It was blasphemy! God doesn't like music. The Quran isn't poetry! Music and art are children of the devil!" The argument was so typical it seemed almost petulant.

"Come on, how do you know that? Did God tell you?" Javed Gul uttered the words very gently, as if cajoling a child in the throes of a tantrum. He just needed to be safe until the guards arrived. Too late. Rashid obviously didn't appreciate being spoken to in such a tone. He fired another shot, and this time he didn't miss.

Javed Gul felt as if he was on fire. Again. But this fire was too real to be exciting. As the door flung open and the guards charged in, an excruciating pain in his right leg radiated upwards, making it impossible to keep standing. He fell to the floor, infinitely appreciative of the plush carpet under his cheek. In a haze he heard more gunshots, and the thought that he would have to pay for damage to the room flitted across his mind. He was amazed at his own bravado, his stupidity. Had he really walked in alone and tried to convert a would-be assassin? Where was his sense of self-preservation?

In a moment of clarity and wisdom accelerated by the agony in his thigh, Javed Gul realized that he had not felt this alive in two years. Although he had not known it, Shamsi's murder had left a gaping hole of mental anguish in his heart that had numbed him beyond words. Perhaps he had rushed into this room because he felt guilty for being spared when his friend had lost his life. Who knew what motivates a human mind – his own or Rashid's?

Rashid! He came back to the present and peered around. His eyes had adjusted to the dark, and he saw that Rashid had proven no match for the hefty guns of the security guards. The poor cameraman lay dead on the carpet just a few feet away from him, his scowl frozen into perpetuity by his own actions.

The pain in Javed Gul's body was getting stronger, and he realized that he was going to faint. Around him he heard a receding wave of sounds: one of the guards calling Harris urgently on his phone; the siren of an ambulance in the distance; an infinitely memorable feminine voice asking if he was alright. With his last ounce of strength, just before he faded into oblivion, he opened his eyes to see Nazia looming over him, a look of worry on her face that no reporter should feel for her interviewee. *I really have to get her phone number.*

A Mother's Heart

Lahore, Pakistan

The phone was ringing, an incessant jarring sound that dragged Farzana out of a deep slumber. She stirred fitfully, not wanting her dream to end, but the phone's dissonant peals were too loud to ignore for long. She arose wearily and picked up the cordless receiver from her bed side table. This better be good, she grumbled to herself.

"Hello?" Her voice was tired but firm. If it was another crank caller asking whether her refrigerator was running, she was prepared to let out a string of profanities, despite her age. Was there no end to the crass behavior of the younger generation?

"*Ammi*, it's me, Asifa. You weren't sleeping, were you?" No surprise, it was her younger daughter, always calling at the wrong time.

"Well, yes, actually I *was* sleeping, dear." Farzana peered at the clock on the wall. Although the room was dark, the clock face was thankfully illuminated. "It's after midnight, you know."

"Oh my God, I'm so sorry, *Ammi*. I can never get used to the time difference between us." Was it Farzana's imagination or did Asifa's apology seem somewhat insincere? "It's the middle of the day here in Chicago, and I just picked up the phone to call you without thinking. Go back to sleep, I'll call you tomorrow."

If she hadn't been half asleep, Farzana would have been annoyed even further at this disregard. How was she supposed to go back to sleep just like that? She slid on her slippers, picked up the light woolen shawl lying on the cane chair next to her bed and walked out slowly to the living room. It was a wide space, filled with heavy furniture reminiscent of a bygone era. These days people preferred lighter furniture, not the pure wood and painted surfaces Farzana surrounded herself with. "No need, dear. I'm awake now. Go ahead and tell me what's on your mind."

"Nothing, I just wanted to see how you were doing." Asifa's voice seemed even less sincere now to Farzana. She doubted that her daughter had called at this hour just to ask about her health. Even for Chicago it was an inconvenient time. She could hear the clanging of pots and pans in the background, as if food was being prepared. Screams of her grandchildren were audible as they ran around the house unchecked.

"I'm fine, *beti*. My knees were giving me trouble again so I decided to go to bed early tonight." Farzana smoothed her silvery hair behind her neck with one hand as she seated herself on a wide sofa covered in faded linen. She stifled a yawn and changed the subject. She never liked talking about her problems, even to her children.

"You know, I was dreaming about your father, may Allah grant him a high place in heaven." As soon as Farzana said the words, she regretted them. Asifa was not the biggest fan of her recently deceased father.

As expected, Asifa sniffed loudly at her mother's pronouncement. "Humph! It'll take more than a few prayers for *Abba* to land in heaven. I don't understand why you're always talking about him. He used to treat you so badly, *Ammi*. You should be glad you don't have to deal with all that screaming and shouting anymore."

There was an incredulous silence as Farzana digested the statement. By now she should be used to Asifa saying such things about Munir. That he had been a harsh man was no secret to anybody, not even the neighbors who could hear his loud tirades at all hours of the day. And Asifa had always had a contentious relationship with him for as long as Farzana could remember. But for a daughter to say such things about her own father just six months after his death was inappropriate and insensitive. To make matters worse, Asifa wasn't alone in these cruel sentiments. Whenever her older son Kamran called from New Jersey he expressed a similar opinion, not seeming to understand how much he hurt his elderly mother.

Was there any point in scolding Asifa for this attitude? Farzana decided to ignore her daughter's crudeness. "Anyway, tell me how the kids are doing. Has Umar gotten over his cold yet? And did Amina find her lost pacifier?" Her mild questions had the desired effect. Asifa forgot her complaints against her dead father and launched into the latest news about her young twins. Farzana sighed. Her daughter was a very intelligent girl, but lately her world seemed to revolve solely around her family. Farzana, who had always been busy with several projects while her own children were growing up, couldn't understand this homebody attitude.

Out of her two offspring, Asifa had been the problem child, Farzana reminisced as she sat in her living room in the middle of the night. She and Munir had spent a considerable amount of money putting their younger daughter through accounting school in Lahore, but Asifa had never actually worked in her chosen field. A few months after graduation, she had accepted a proposal from a class fellow named Samiullah, bound for the United States to obtain a PhD. Knowing full well that good proposals were hard to find, her parents had agreed to the marriage. Pregnant almost immediately afterwards, Asifa never got the chance to practice her accounting skills in her new country, preferring to stay home to tend to her son Umar and daughter Amina. The three year-olds were little terrors in Farzana's opinion, no different from all the other Americans who had no respect for their elders. But Asifa adored them and spent hours talking about their allegedly cute behavior to anybody who would take note.

Today was no exception. Farzana listened to the escapades of the little terrors with half an ear, making noncommittal sounds at intervals. Umar's cold had developed into a fever and cough, and Amina's pacifier had been found behind the trash can for the fiftieth time. She was horrified at this display of lazy motherhood. Had Asifa lost all her common sense? She considered sharing some home remedies for both the cold and the pacifier, but decided against it. She was sure that her daughter wouldn't be interested in her advice. Like all expatriate Pakistanis, Asifa thought she and her American doctors knew more than the combined wisdom of older generations brought up on eastern medicine.

With the phone wedged between her right ear and shoulder, Farzana picked up the enormous television remote. Her older son Kamran had bought this new flat-screen set for her during his visit for Munir's funeral, and she still hadn't figured out what all the buttons on the remote were for. Thankfully, tonight she was able to switch on the television at the first try. She missed her little TV with the five buttons on the front – power, volume up, volume down, channel up and channel down. What else did one really need to watch a good show? It had worked perfectly for seventeen years, but she had been forced to sell it when the new gift arrived: a fancy internet-ready smart television with a remote so big she often mistook it for her cordless phone. Totally useless, in Farzana's opinion.

Asifa was still talking about the twins, unaware that her mother was listening with less than rapt attention. Truth be told, Farzana was hardly listening at all. With the volume muted, she switched channels until she found a late-night talk show she particularly liked. She wondered what the topic was that day. Something scandalous, she was sure. The show was extremely popular due to its juicy subjects and racy hosts, and Farzana suddenly wished her daughter would end the conversation so she could watch in peace. "*Beti*, I'm really tired, I should probably go back to sleep now," she told Asifa firmly, interrupting a monologue about the twins' recent tantrum in a shopping center.

Asifa was immediately contrite. With more apologies, she said her goodbyes, and Farzana was finally left alone to enjoy her show. She turned the volume up. One of the advantages of being a widow was that she could listen to the television as loud as she wanted, without angry complaints from her husband in the next room. The first guest had already been called to the stage; a small-time politician who had been discovered in a prostitute's home during a police raid. As the beleaguered young man sputtered and spewed all manners of excuses for his presence at such a shameful place, the heavily made up young show host showed pictures of his arrest on the big screen behind her. The audience stamped their feet and booed loudly, adding to the raucous and giving voice to their low opinions of elected officials.

Farzana watched avidly until the first commercial break. The host, her clothes more appropriate for a wedding than a television program, announced the next guest waiting back stage: a *maulvi* who would no doubt expound upon the myriad of sins associated with extramarital sex. That was bound to be a heckle-inducing segment, thought Farzana with anticipation. And who knew who the third guest, traditionally a surprise on the show, would be. The prostitute herself, perhaps? Farzana wouldn't resist rubbing her hands with glee.

She got up from the sofa and shuffled slowly to the kitchen to make herself a cup of tea while the commercials ran. The kitchen floor was freezing; her knees could tell that winter was close. Lahore could get bitterly cold by the end of the year, but it was still September so she had some time to plan. She should buy new socks, she told herself, and maybe even a new sweater if she could find a good bargain. Asifa could probably send her a nice cashmere sweater from Chicago if she asked, but she didn't like asking her children for anything. They had a tendency to lord it over their mother for the longest time. In any case, the quality of wool in Pakistan was much better than in those western countries, anyway. She put the matter to rest in her mind. She would take a trip to the local market on the weekend and select some suitable winter clothing with neither of her children any wiser.

The kettle whistled. She let the water boil while she went about the comfortable routine of making tea. Teabags, mugs, milk, a tiny bit of sugar; she made two teas before she remembered that Munir wasn't alive to be sharing it with her anymore. The simple fact of his absence in this longstanding ritual affected her deeply. Tears filled her eyes and she sat down on the closest dining chair to compose herself. It was strange how she felt a strong emotional connection to Munir at the oddest times now that he was gone, although their relationship during his lifetime had been tenuous at best. The most unexpected of actions turned on the waterworks: perusing a recipe book and coming across a description of his favorite lamp chops; watching television and hearing the voice of the newscaster he despised; seeing a beggar on the street and being reminded of the coins he kept in the ashtray of their car for those poor souls.

She wiped her eyes with the edge of the woolen shawl, her face wrinkled with age and fatigue. She felt slightly foolish to be crying, even more so for being embarrassed about it. Her husband had just died, for God's sake! She had every right to bawl her eyes out anytime she felt like it. They had been married for thirty nine years, planning a fortieth anniversary party, until a car accident in March had ended their relationship in an instant. Just like that, without the opportunity to say good bye or "I'm sorry". Asifa was right, he hadn't been the easiest person to live with, but he had still been her husband, her companion, and she missed him. Being alone at this stage of life was such a daunting notion that she would have preferred an abusive husband to none at all.

Farzana shook her head strongly to dispel her morose thoughts. She was not one to waste her tears on useless emotion. She straightened her aching back, poured the extra mug of tea down the kitchen drain and took her own steaming mug into the living room to watch her talk show. It was almost one o'clock in the morning, a few minutes from the rerun of her favorite Turkish soap. With so many people appearing to offer condolences during the last few months, she had missed a lot of television. She decided she was lucky that Asifa had woken her up tonight. She could finally catch up with all her favorite shows in one marathon sitting and lots of tea.

And watch television she did, reveling in her newfound freedom that allowed her to stay up as late as she wanted and watch any program she liked. Munir had usually objected to her choice of shows, but now, at the age of sixty five, she was finally her own mistress. How sad that liberty had come at the expense of her husband's life. Regardless, she had a lot of television to watch. She decided to put on another kettle of water to boil.

* * *

At ten in the morning, Farzana was rudely awakened by banging on the front door. She looked around and realized that she had fallen asleep stretched out on the sofa in front of the television. Great! Now her neck was rigid and sure to hurt for days. She shuffled to the front door slowly, ignoring the continuous knocking, and took her time unlocking the two padlocks that kept her safe from robbers. Her maidservant Mary was standing outside, reporting for her daily duties much earlier than usual. Curse the girl for being on time today of all days, thought a bleary eyed Farzana as she swung the door open and allowed Mary to enter. "Why are you so impatient?" She demanded. "Don't you know it takes me a long time to come to the door? Your hammering isn't going to make my old bones move any faster."

"I'm sorry, *Baji*, I thought maybe you were asleep and couldn't hear me. I went to church for mass early this morning, so I was able to get here early. I hope I didn't wake you."

Mary didn't sound sorry. She was close to Asifa in age and very much like her in attitude as well. These young people! Farzana said the words in her mind as if they were an expletive. The older she got, the more the young seemed to irritate her with their impatience and sense of superiority. They seemed to have no appreciation for the fact that wisdom came with age and experience. Mary was in her late twenties, very smug about her job in Farzana's household and constantly making demands upon her employer. While Munir had been alive, he would often loan her money or allow her to go on extended vacations while Farzana fumed in silence. Now with her protector gone, Mary was about to get a rude awakening.

"Get started with the sweeping while I go to the bathroom," she told Mary sternly as she shuffled away. "And as soon as you're done, I need you to iron my new *shalwar kameez*, the blue one with the tie-die *dupatta*. I'm going to go to the clinic this afternoon and I want to look my best."

The morning passed quickly. Mary, despite her shortcomings, was a hard worker, and after almost ten years of service could do the job with her eyes closed. Mornings were reserved for house cleaning – sweeping the perpetual dust that seemed to envelop the house and its furnishings, mopping the floors with a strong chemical to preserve the shine, wiping clean every table top and accessory until it gleamed. Close to noon she would start preparations for lunch, and while the food was cooking she would wash the dirty dishes by hand. Afternoons were spent washing clothes and ironing clean ones. She didn't leave until four o'clock, when it was time for her own children to return from school.

Now that Farzana was virtually alone, there wasn't as much cooking, ironing or washing to do. She remembered when Asifa had been single and living in Lahore with them – was that only four years ago? The dishes would really pile up then, and every day there would be a new request for a special dish for lunch or dessert. Mutton *pulao,* vegetable kabob, *aaloo gosht* – Mary was an excellent cook and they all used to enjoy her creations. Despite her irritation at her daughter's habits, Farzana often missed her laughter now that she was gone. On the other hand, life now seemed serene by contrast, not just for her but for Mary as well.

Thinking back to happier times improved her mood considerably, and her annoyance with Mary abated by late morning. She called the maidservant to her room to give her a neck massage and braid her thinning silver hair. She was lonely, and a hardworking maidservant was better than no one at all. Often in the afternoons, when all work was done, Mary would read the newspaper to her or relate the latest gossip from the tabloids. Today, she sang an Urdu poem while she massaged, soothing Farzana's headache more effectively than any medication.

Feeling revived after the massage, Farzana proceeded to change into freshly ironed new clothes. She was going to the clinic for the first time after Munir's death, and she didn't want any pitying glances. New clothes always gave her a boost of confidence, something she was desperately feeling the need for after her long night. She was just finishing up when, promptly at eleven-thirty, the phone rang shrilly once again. It was probably her first-born son

Kamran, a doctor in New Jersey who called faithfully every day at the same time.

She hurried to pick it up; if she was too slow and the phone stopped ringing, Kamran would get worried and start calling their relatives in an effort to find out what had happened. She muttered under her breath. Didn't he realize that she may have other things to do at eleven-thirty? It wasn't fair to expect her to stay beside the phone every day out of regard for his feelings.

"Hello." She was out of breath but she had reached the phone in time. "Kamran, is that you?"

"Yes *Ammi*, it's me. *Assalamo alaikum!* Why are you panting? Is everything okay?" He was, as usual, suspicious about every little thing.

"I'm fine, son, *Wa alaikum assalam!* I was in the bathroom and had to run to the phone. I'm just a little winded, that's all." She sat down on edge of the bed and rested against the pillows, waiting for her heart to stop pounding. She didn't want to tell him, but recently any kind of exercise left her feeling breathless and exhausted. "You tell me, how are you? How's everything going at your job?"

"I'm fine, the job is fine." He sounded annoyed. "You shouldn't run in the bathroom, *Ammi*, you know that. You could fall down and get seriously hurt. Why can't you get a cell phone? That way you can pick up wherever you are."

Farzana sighed dramatically. Not this conversation again. How many times had he offered to buy her a cell phone and how many times had she refused? "I'm too old for a cell phone, son," she explained gently as if speaking to a small child. "I don't have pockets, so I can't carry it around with me everywhere I go. I would still have to leave it on the table whenever I went to the bathroom because it's just too weird to be carrying a phone there. I'm just fine with my cordless telephone, just be patient with me. Let the phone ring for a long time and eventually I'll reach it."

"Okay, as you wish. Anyway, how is the pain in your chest? Feeling better after the change in medicine?"

"Yes dear, I'm doing very well. There hasn't been any pain now for quite some time. I'm glad you were able to review the scans and make sure everything was fine. I don't trust the doctors here, always trying to make a quick buck."

She was truly grateful that Kamran had decided to become a doctor, although his current career path was less than desirable to her. After graduating from medical school, he had gone to New Jersey for his residency seven years ago, and never looked back. To make matters worse for his parents, he had married an American colleague, a *gori*, and Munir had felt especially betrayed. There had been plenty of long distance fighting and cursing; in one argument, Kamran had vowed never to return home. Farzana had been crushed, a blameless victim of two male egos. Yet the bond between mother and son endured, and he maintained his practice of phoning her at the same time each morning. He was a good son, she thought fondly, even if she didn't always agree with his decisions, and almost never followed his non-medical advice.

"*Ammi*, I was thinking..." His voice trailed off, as if he didn't know how she would react.

"What, *beta*?" She prompted him. His voice sounded more and more like Munir's every day. When he had come to Lahore for the funeral she had noticed that he resembled Munir more than ever before. Thankfully, that was the extent of their similarities. Her husband had been a handsome man, but his temper had not endeared him to people. Kamran, on the other hand, was friendly and soft spoken, making a conscious attempt not to make the same mistakes as his father had.

Kamran seemed to be thinking about Munir as well. "Now that *Abba* has died, why don't you move here with me? I really worry about you being there in Pakistan all by yourself. It's no place for an old lady, you know that."

Farzana was suddenly incensed. Who was he calling an old lady? She wondered why he was offering this proposition today, just a week after he had announced the happy news that he and his wife Jessica were expecting their first baby. "No!" she said more forcefully than she had intended. "This is my home, I'm not moving away from here. And especially not to a country like America!"

"What's wrong with America? It's a great place to live, and you'll be close to your family. Asifa's not far from us either. Don't you want to spend the rest of your days with us?"

"Rest of my days? Are you expecting me to die soon?" She wished he had not called that day. Her headache was back with a vengeance, reminding her that she hadn't slept more than a few hours last night. She pledged never to stay up all night watching those idiotic television shows again.

"No *Ammi*, of course not!" Kamran seemed genuinely horrified at the prospect of her death. "You know we love you, we want you to be comfortable in your old age. Why would you want to live in Pakistan all alone? What's keeping you there? Lahore isn't the safe place it used to be, you know. It's becoming as dangerous as Karachi."

"Dangerous or not, this is my home. I can't start a new life somewhere else at this age. Over here I can drive, I can go wherever I want, when I want. I know the roads, the neighborhoods. I have a few friends and relatives left. What would I do there in New Jersey, sitting at home where it snows half the year?" To Farzana, it was indeed a terrible picture: housebound, ailing, dependent on a *gori*.

Kamran sounded impatient. "It doesn't snow here half the year. I've told you this before. It's very beautiful most of the time."

He paused, then went on more gently. "In fact, right now it's autumn and the trees look so beautiful: red, yellow, orange. People actually drive up here from other states to look at the fall colors. *Ammi*, you would love it here, I'm telling you."

"Well, I'm sure it's beautiful. Thank you for the offer, but I'm not interested."

"It's not a matter of interest, *Ammi*. It's about safety. I worry about you all the time over there. You could fall in the middle of the night and nobody would know. Or someone could break into the house again, like last year. Or you could be out shopping when a bomb explodes. That country is no longer safe, and being old and alone, it's even more risky for you."

Farzana knew he was just being protective, the new head of the household now that his father was gone. Still, she didn't appreciate his bossy attitude. What had the world come to, when sons ordered their mothers around? But she was in no mood to fight, not today. "Okay, okay, I'll think about it." She placated him even though she had no intention of moving. Maybe he would forget about it in a few days. She decided it was time to talk about something else.

"I forgot to tell you, a man from Kamiaab Bank called two days ago. He said something about your father's savings, but I don't think your father had an account there. He said it's a very substantial amount. He wanted me to come down to the branch and sign some papers. What should I do?" Farzana knew any mention of Munir would make Kamran sit up and take notice. In any case, she didn't know too much about finance, so she really did need his advice.

"Kamiaab Bank? I've never heard of it. Why didn't you tell me this before?" As she had expected, he was sufficiently diverted, not unlike the many times as a child when she handed him a toffee to distract him from something else he wanted. "*Ammi*, please don't sign anything. You know what people are like; this man is probably trying to swindle you. Tell him to give you all the paperwork and account information, and fax it to me. I'll have my friend Sohail in Rawalpindi take a look. You remember Sohail, don't you? He's vice president of ..."

"Yes, yes, I remember." Farzana glanced at the clock on the wall behind her. She was going to be late for the clinic if she didn't leave soon. "*Beta*, I have to go now. I'll talk to you later."

"Wait, where are you going?"

"I have to go to the clinic; it's my regular day to volunteer. I'll be back in a little while." Farzana knew he wouldn't like this. Neither Munir nor Kamran had approved of her volunteer work at the neighborhood clinic. Despite their differences, they were more alike than they had ever admitted.

She was right. Kamran launched another lecture. "Don't tell me you're still going to that awful place, *Ammi*! One of these days you're going to catch some terrible disease. Why do you need to go there today, with your heart still on the mend?"

Farzana laughed inwardly. Her son, a doctor whose specialty was treating sick children, was objecting to his mother working at a children's clinic. It was the height of absurdity. His need to control her was reminiscent of her late husband's and she did not appreciate it. She may be old, but her advancing age didn't make her any less independent or intelligent.

"Yes, I still work there, Kamran. I feel needed over there, and I know I'm doing something worthwhile, something rewarding. It's perfectly safe, they have guards there, and I always clean my hands thoroughly with antibacterial lotion afterwards. And my chest is fine now. I told you it hasn't hurt in several days. Don't worry about me, *beta*. I have to leave now, okay? I'll wait for your call tomorrow. *Khuda Hafiz!*"

Without waiting for an answer, Farzana put the receiver down slowly and deliberately. She was so tired of justifying her actions to her children. Surely she had earned the right to make her own decisions? She would have worried about this some more, but she really was late. Even though she was given no specific arrival time by the clinic staff, she liked being punctual in all aspects of her life. It amazed people around her; most people in Lahore didn't care the slightest about being on time for anything. But she held herself to a higher standard, reminiscent of an earlier era.

Minutes later, dressed in her new suit, car keys in hand, she left the house, giving last-minute instructions to Mary to buy some potatoes and okra when the vegetable cart came around to their street. Her maidservant may be irritating, but she was a trustworthy young woman. In this day and age, few servants could be trusted alone in the house, and Mary was one of them.

The morning was crisp, with just a hint of a cool breeze. Farzana drove her rickety old Nissan carefully, steering clear of the big roads with their heavy traffic. Her eyesight wasn't what it used to be and sometimes she misjudged distances. The car was too old to go very fast, anyway. It took her fifteen minutes to reach the clinic; a younger person would have reached it in five. The clinic was situated across two main roads in a commercial area dotted with shops of all kinds. Twenty years ago when it had opened, this part of town had been much quieter. Now, with a main bus stop across the street, it seemed to have become a major thoroughfare. With the bus came an influx of patients from all parts of the city. One doctor and three nurses worked here full-time, and several medical students volunteered to gain valuable experience. Farzana was truly delighted to be associated with such a worthy organization.

She entered the mosaicked hallway of the clinic and was met by Naeema, the receptionist. Only nineteen years old with a four month-old baby whom she brought with her to the clinic every day, Naeema seemed to be in a constant state of nervousness. Today, however, she seemed even more anxious than usual. "Farzana Aunty, where have you been? You were supposed to be here at twelve-thirty. Everyone's waiting for you."

Farzana was bewildered. Who was waiting for her? What on earth was going on? Nobody had cared much about her being late before. She felt a moment of dread. A new administrator had been hired a month ago and he was much stricter than his predecessor. Surely he wasn't going to fire an old volunteer for being half an hour late? Could he even fire someone who wasn't being paid?

She hesitantly followed Naeema to the end of the hallway where a door leading to one of the meeting rooms lay ominously closed. Naeema opened the door with a flourish and pushed her inside. It was dark and Farzana's bespectacled eyes took a few seconds to adjust. She had time to make out a few bulky shapes before the lights went on and a huge roar of "Congratulations!" filled the air. She felt her heart begin to palpitate at this shock and she put her palms against her chest to steady the pumping. She blinked rapidly; she still couldn't understand what was going on.

A kindly hand steadied her. It was Mr. Fazal, the new administrator. Just over forty, with short cropped black hair and a trimmed goatee, he was young and smart and reportedly from an influential Lahori family. From the prattle of the other volunteers, Farzana had learned that he held a degree in business administration, exactly what the clinic needed to make it more successful. She had never spoken to him before, never realized what a kind, smiling face he had.

"Farzana Aunty, you are finally here!" Mr. Fazal declared in a polished, accentless voice. It seemed as if everyone from the youngest patient to the oldest janitor called her Aunty. If she hadn't been truly old she would have felt offended at this liberty. She concentrated on what the administrator was saying.

"I can see from the look on your face that you weren't expecting this surprise party!" He seemed genuinely amused. Farzana looked around in astonishment. The room was full of people – patients she had helped over the years, neighbors, volunteers and staff. Even those who had moved to other jobs at other organizations were here. Had they all really come just to meet her? It was unbelievable.

"Don't you remember that today is your twenty-fifth anniversary with the clinic?" Mr. Fazal reminded her gently. He was still holding on to her arm, perhaps suspecting that she might fall if left unsupported. He turned to the guests and raised his hand to request silence. "Ladies and gentlemen! As you all know, Farzana Aunty has been with us from the time this clinic was created, maybe even before that. It was she who decided to bring some ladies together and raise funds for medical care in this neighborhood. It was she who was the true inspiration and the driving force behind the clinic itself. At that time we were all volunteer-based, even the doctors and nurses. In fact, Farzana Aunty's own brother, the late Dr. Mahmood, volunteered here five days a week for two years until we raised enough money to hire someone. And she herself has been volunteering here every week for the last twenty five years. I think she deserves some serious applause!"

The room erupted in claps and whistles. Farzana was moved to tears – happy tears, for being appreciated for who she was. She fleetingly recalled the ugly arguments over the years with Munir regarding her involvement at the clinic. He was always jealous of the time she spent there, the love she poured into the patients who entered its doorways. She dabbed her eyes with the edge of her tie-dyed *dupatta* and smiled tremulously. "Thank you, everyone. This is such a surprise and a great honor for me. I am really so grateful to all of you who are here today. This clinic has been a life-saver for me. It gave me a sense of purpose and a feeling of independence.

Please believe me when I say that I have gained so much by volunteering here."

Another long applause, then Mr. Fazal led her gently to one side of the room where a table was laid with all types of delicious food. When had they planned all this? she wondered with pleasure. This really proved they loved her, considered her a part of the extended clinic family. She sat down on a nearby seat with a plate full of food. She had to eat carefully because of her heart condition, but she would definitely enjoy the company, she told herself. Immediately, a hoard of patients surrounded her, talking loudly and cheerfully.

There was Sumera, who had been coming in for influenza shots each year since the age of two. Seven years old now, Sumera rushed to her beloved Farzana Aunty who always held her hand during the injections, wiped her tears afterwards and rewarded her with a huge lollipop. There was little Amir, not so little anymore, who had been brought in with chicken pox ten or eleven years ago. Farzana had visited him at home every week while he was sick, reading to him and feeding him soup while his mother attended to her household chores. There were countless other patients who remembered the kindly Aunty as a comforting soul during their illnesses, and had come to pay their respects and offer their gratitude for her long years of service. Farzana was stunned at this show of affection, and after all the heartache of the last few months, her heart blossomed under their attention.

An hour later, when all the hugs, kisses, congratulations and tears were spent, the crowd finally began to disperse. Farzana was getting sleepy. She was too old for so much excitement, she thought, and decided to leave as well. Mary would be waiting for her to return, and another massage would be very welcome. Picking up her purse, fixing her glasses atop her nose, and adjusting her *dupatta*, she waved her goodbyes and shuffled out the door.

Mr. Fazal stopped her at the clinic exit. "Farzana Aunty! I hope you liked the party!" He was obviously pleased at the way the event had turned out.

"Yes, thank you so much!" Farzana realized she hadn't thanked him personally for the tribute. He must think her so rude. She hastened to assure him of her eternal gratitude. "It was a wonderful party, and of course I was completely surprised. You should be glad I didn't suffer a heart attack!" She wiggled her finger at him in mock seriousness, but smiled to show she was only joking.

He relaxed. "Yes, I heard you've been having heart problems recently. That's understandable considering your age." He paused delicately and she sensed that he was trying to say something without upsetting her, almost like Kamran had done earlier that day over the phone. "That's actually why I decided to have a big party for your anniversary. If you feel that you need to retire from the clinic, we will all completely understand."

Farzana felt as if the earth was shaking under her feet. "Retire?" she repeated uncomprehending.

He bit his lip under the goatee. "Please don't take this the wrong way, Aunty. You will always be welcome here. I just wanted to give you that option. You have dedicated your life to this clinic, and now that Munir Uncle has passed away I understand that you may not want to stay here anymore..."

She jumped at this suggestion, ready for a fight. "What do you mean? Who told you I may not be staying here in Lahore?" she demanded fiercely. "This is my home, where else would I go?"

Mr. Fazal was clearly regretting his decision to talk to her. Nevertheless, he continued on respectfully, "Nobody told me anything, Aunty. I just assumed that you wouldn't want to live here alone, at your age. You are blessed to have two children living in America. Anyone else would have moved long ago. Please Aunty, don't be offended."

Farzana glared at him suspiciously, no longer assured of his sincerity. What audacity to suggest that she should retire! After all the time she had spent at the clinic, she truly considered it her second home. For him to suggest that they no longer needed her was preposterous and secretly a little heartbreaking. He continued his excuses, but she waved away his words and left the building as fast as her aching knees would carry her.

She approached her car with hot tears pouring down her wrinkled face and her chest beginning its familiar squeeze. This clinic had been her last bastion of hope against encroaching senility and loneliness. If she couldn't come here every other day, where would she go? If she had wanted to retire, wouldn't she have let them know? The anniversary celebration that she had so cherished an hour ago now simply appeared to be a forced farewell party. She felt like screaming out in anger and pain, but out of habit she remained silent. After long minutes, waiting for the tightness in her chest to subside, she opened her purse to look for her car keys.

"Mrs. Farzana Munir?" A voice just behind her startled her mightily, and she almost dropped her purse. She looked up fearfully. Robbery was a very real danger in Lahore, even in broad daylight. A young man dressed in a black blazer and trousers stood behind her, smiling an enormously toothy and phony smile. She was confused; a robber wouldn't be smiling, would he?

"I'm Shahrukh Ali, from Kamiaab Bank. I talked to you on the phone two days ago." His voice was certainly familiar, but she continued to look at him questioningly. Too much had happened to her emotionally today, and she was not as quick in her head as she should be.

"Yes, I remember that name," she agreed slowly. "What are you doing here? How did you know I'd be here?"

"I went to your house. Your maid told me where you were." His answer was smooth, but Farzana wasn't born yesterday. She was positive that Mary would never tell a stranger the address of her clinic. Who was this man and what did he really want?

"Can I help you with something?" She asked pointedly, trying to put on a brave front despite her hammering heart. Never would she show this man that she was anything less than fully confident. "What's so urgent that you need to follow me around?"

"I explained to you over the phone that your husband had an account with us; a savings account worth more than twenty *lakh* rupees. Now that he has died we need to complete the paperwork and transfer the account over to you."

What he was saying didn't make any sense to Farzana. She struggled to understand. "My husband had twenty *lakh* rupees stashed at your bank? That's impossible. He was a government officer, he never made that much money."

"Oh, I'm sure he made that money somehow. The stock market, perhaps?" The man's grin was getting wider, uglier. "What does it matter how he made the money? The point is that it's yours now, and we are anxious to hand it over to you as soon as possible."

Farzana did not believe that sentence for a moment. Despite the growing pain in her chest and the irregular breathing that secretly insisted she was not as well as she told everyone, she pressed on stubbornly. If Shahrukh Ali was a criminal, he would soon see she was not one to be trifled with. She leaned back against her car to gain some strength, both physical and mental.

"Well, even if all that money is indeed my husband's, how did you know that he had died? At his regular bank I had to inform them about his death and run after them for weeks to accept his death certificate, even bribe the bankers to release his savings to me." She should have been highly satisfied with her deduction, but all she could think was that she needed to sit down.

Shahrukh's smile slipped. "Listen, you old lady! You may not believe it, but your husband did have an account with us. He had several dealings with us over the last few years. There's a lot of money at stake here, and I'm not letting you get in the way. If you won't sign these papers, you'll regret it!"

Farzana realized in terror that he was serious. As if his snarly voice and glittering eyes weren't terrifying enough, he held up his hand and showed her a big knife. Even if she hadn't been sixty five she would have capitulated. As it were, her heart was pounding so loudly in her chest she thought she would throw up. The pain in her chest was getting infinitely worse. She breathed erratically as he came closer, holding up a pen and some papers. He shoved her towards her car and ordered "sign here!"

Gasping heavily, she complied. He made her sign several times on a blank piece of paper until he was satisfied with the result. She realized that he was probably going to use her signature to forge documents and steal the twenty *lakhs* for himself. She didn't care as much about the money as she did about her physical wellbeing. What was he planning to do with her?

His mission accomplished, he pushed Farzana to the ground. Although she was frail and weighed not more than fifty kilograms, she hit the pavement with force and her glasses smashed underneath her. She worried that he would kill her with the knife, but he fled as quietly as he had arrived, probably not considering her a real threat. She should have been grateful that her life had been spared, but her chest was squeezed so tightly that she could hardly breathe and a deep pain radiated from her left arm. Is this what a heart attack feels like? she wondered faintly as she succumbed to the pain, and fell back unconscious.

◦ ◦ ◦

For the next few days, Farzana weaved in and out of consciousness. She vaguely understood that she was in a hospital, hooked up to machines. Her entire body ached mightily, and her throat was parched all the time. She saw glimpses of people she knew – Mr. Fazal from the clinic once, her cousin Saeed and his wife a few times. She saw Mary sitting frequently at her side, Bible in hand, praying. Was she that sick? Was she dying? She wanted answers but she couldn't find the strength to keep her eyes open for more than a few seconds.

One time she thought she heard Munir's angry voice. Was it just a dream or had she died? Surely she wouldn't feel such exhaustion after death. The voice grew stronger, and Farzana tried to focus. It wasn't Munir, it sounded more like her son Kamran. But how was that possible? Kamran was in New Jersey, wasn't he?

"I don't care what your policy is. I'm a qualified doctor, probably more qualified than you, and I need to see her charts. If you don't comply, I will speak with your administrator!" Yes, she thought, that was definitely Kamran, although his tone was more like his father's than she had ever heard. Why was he so furious? Curiosity got the better of her, and she willed her eyes open, pleasantly surprised to instinctively sense that she was much stronger. Kamran was standing at her bedside with another doctor; they were obviously discussing her health.

Farzana must have made a sound, because they both turned simultaneously and looked at her. "*Ammi!*" gasped Kamran, immediately softening his tone. "How are you feeling now? We've all been so worried!"

She tried to speak, but her throat was parched. Mary came forward from the shadows and offered her a glass of water, her face almost as creased as her clothes. Farzana saw she was wearing the same green patterned *shalwar kameez* she had last arrived at her house in. Had her maidservant not gone home in all these days? Farzana drank it gratefully, uncaring that most of it spilled down the front of her hospital gown. Feeling much better, she looked at

Kamran sternly. "I'm all right, but what are you doing here? Is this a dream?"

Kamran laughed, grateful that his mother was feeling well enough to berate him. She had never been one to feel pity for herself or seek sympathy from others. "I'm really here. You had a heart attack when someone accosted you in the clinic parking lot and Mr. Fazal called me immediately. I came here on the next flight. What did you think, that I didn't care about you enough to come take care of you?"

Farzana didn't want to admit that she did think exactly that about her children. Neither Asifa nor Kamran had ever expressed their emotions, preferring to complain and give impossible suggestions as soon as they reached adolescence. Farzana now realized that the suggestions weren't as impossible as she had considered them. After all, their family had lived together all those years in a continuous state of quarrel, and both the children had fled the toxic environment of their home as soon as humanly possible. Neither she nor Munir had taught them by their own example how to express affection. She was relieved to witness that, despite it all, they had somehow managed to build happy lives as adults, incorporating the concepts of duty and responsibility towards their parents.

All of a sudden Farzana felt ashamed. Ashamed of thinking the worst of her own children, ashamed of assuming that they didn't want what was best or her. Despite her efforts, she felt tears welling up inside her. She was so happy to see him, her son, her pride and joy. He had risen from the ashes of their ordinary existence, fought the chains of an abusive father, and reached the height of his profession in a way that most Pakistanis could only dream about. Yet he still made time every day to call his elderly mother, worried about her constantly, and now he had dropped everything to fly half way across the world to be at her side. Why had she ever thought he was controlling or uncaring?

Kamran still had one more surprise for his mother. He opened the door to the hospital room and beckoned to someone outside. A minute later a tall, dark haired, young woman walked in shyly. She was dressed in the traditional *shalwar kameez* but the clothes didn't seem to fit quite right. Farzana peered with tired eyes at this new face, unknown yet familiar. Only when the young woman said "Salaam, *Ammi*" her accent gave her away and Farzana finally understood who she was. It was Jessica, her American daughter-in-law. The dam broke and she sobbed as she hugged Jessica, who wasn't as white as she had envisioned. If this young woman could come all this way in her pregnancy to visit her husband's mother in the hospital, surely Farzana could find it in her heart to accept her into the family with open arms.

The three spent the day talking quietly, Farzana regaling a fascinated Jessica with stories from Kamran's childhood. Mary and the doctor hovered around, trying to ensure that Farzana didn't exert herself, but she waved them both away. Who knew how long she had to live? There was no time like the present to get acquainted, even discuss the future. Kamran called Asifa on Skype. Farzana was pleased beyond words to see the little terrors' faces much subdued and asking after grandma's health rather earnestly. Even their father, the uncommunicative Samiullah, came on the video for a minute to ask how she was feeling.

Asifa herself looked as if she had been crying ceaselessly, her eyes red and nose scrubbed raw. The evidence of her daughter's pain gave Farzana a perverse kind of satisfaction, glad to see such a visible demonstration of her love for the first time. Funny how it took a heart attack to convince people to reveal what had always been in their hearts.

Kamran, Jessica and Asifa asked tentatively about her plans after she was discharged from the hospital. Rather diffidently she told them that she had made up her mind. If they still wanted her, she would begin the immigration process to move permanently to the United States. The paperwork would of course take some time, enough for her to dispose of her furnishings and talk to some friends to find Mary an alternate place to work. She was also thinking of something else, now that her health was back in sync and she was feeling her old contentious self again.

"*Beta*," she told Kamran. "Do you think you could give Mr. Fazal a telephone call? It's well-known at the clinic that he has connections in the police, and I want to see if he can find the thug who caused my heart attack." She couldn't wait to give that phony liar a piece of her mind and maybe even the beating of his life.

Kamran laughed heartily. He was sitting at her bedside, a rare moment of mother-son conversation while Jessica and Mary went back to Farzana's house for a much-needed rest. "It's good to know you are back to normal, *Ammi*! I can always tell that you're doing fine when you want to give someone a piece of your mind!" He became serious, shaking his head slowly. "I'm not optimistic about catching that crook, though. People like him are a dime a dozen. Who knows if his real name was Sharukh Ali or something else? We don't have any proof, any witnesses, nothing. But I will call Mr. Fazal and see if he can at least file a complaint with the police. I think looking forward to some kind of revenge will keep you strong and hopeful!"

"Okay *beta,* as you wish. I will leave this matter in your hands." If Kamran was amazed at this new attitude, he didn't say anything. Truth be told, Farzana was definitely better, but she had learned something about herself in the last few days. She was no obstinate fool, to dig her feet in the sand despite the scares she had received in the last few days. She was old, but not senile, and she had finally witnessed a glimpse of the inevitable if she remained in Pakistan any longer. It was time to accept defeat.

* * *

Trenton, New Jersey

Her new home is small and cold, a thousand times colder than Lahore. It is snowing outside, and Farzana has decided that she hates the snow. Those idiotic neighborhood children making snowmen and throwing snowballs at each other don't remind her of her own childhood when she and her friends used to make mud pies. No, these children are disrespectful and noisy little miscreants. She wishes she could go outside and give them a piece of her mind, but she knows they will probably call the police.

Grudgingly Farzana admits to herself that the police here are super-efficient and capable. Not like those useless law enforcement officials in Pakistan who couldn't catch a fly if it buzzed right in front of their noses. She is positive that if someone tries to steal her money or accost her in a parking lot in New Jersey, the police will have that person behind bars before nightfall. She is sure of this fact because she has watched the show COPS with avid interest every single day since she arrived in this godforsaken land.

She is still not too keen about America, of course, but there is a peace here that she has never experienced before. At her age, she considers peace the most important requirement of life. The winter here reminds her of the time years ago when she had visited Muree, that quaint little town in the north of Islamabad. She and Munir had stayed there in a little hotel in the shadows of the mountains to celebrate their twentieth wedding anniversary. It was a little piece of heaven, and if she closes her eyes and ignores the American accents of the children outside, she can imagine that she is back in Muree, her annoying but dependable husband by her side.

She hugs herself, feeling cold and alone. She sorely misses her rough old sweater, hating the heavy black coats she has to wear whenever she leaves the house. No, not her house, she corrects herself firmly, Kamran's and Jessica's house. She still doesn't think of it as her home. Perhaps by the time summer comes she will have forgotten Lahore. Perhaps she will feel more at home when the baby is born, anytime now, and she becomes a grandmother once again. Perhaps.

The doorbell rings insistently, and she grumbles under her breath as she gets up to answer it. "Impatient youth! Don't they know my old bones can't move too fast?" She pauses as she remembers how often she used to say the same thing to Mary. She must remember to ask Kamran to call Mr. Fazal and find out how his new maid is doing. She smoothes her hair and straightens her new glasses as she opens the door with a half-smile. Asifa and her twins are standing outside, waiting impatiently to hug, kiss, and tell stories of their journey.

"*Nani, Nani*" they cry with excitement, and Farzana feels a warmth spreading into her heart along with their plump little hands around her neck. She pretends to be angry, but she is smiling. She ushers them all to the fireplace in the living room, to the waiting *chai* and home-made *pakoras* with spicy ketchup. Kamran arrives an hour later from the hospital, bringing gifts for everyone. She is tired by now, but content. After the twins have gone to bed, she will watch the latest episode of her favorite reality talk show on her new satellite television with Asifa, who has recently been converted. Jessica, still learning Urdu, will hopefully join them as well. It isn't Lahore, but it's something.

Making the Team

"*Back up! Back up!* That's the wicket!"

"Show me the ball, man, where's the ball?"

"Call the other guys, why aren't they here yet?"

Nida woke up to loud yells wafting in from the open window of her bedroom. For a moment she lay in bed, wondering what the commotion was all about. She looked groggily at the clock on her desk and registered that it was after nine o'clock in the morning. She was pretty sure it was Saturday. Why was the time on the clock face making her feel as if something was amiss? Then all at once the implication of the shouts outside dawned on her: those darn boys were starting the game early again!

Nida jumped out of bed and landed on her slippers, hastily putting them on while grabbing her clothes from the chair where she had thrown them the night before. As she raced to don her customary long button-down shirt and loose pants, she kept looking out of the window to monitor the activity outside. Her bedroom was on the second floor, so she had the advantage of height to afford her some privacy. Six boys were already gathered outside, preparing to play another weekend game of cricket. If she didn't hurry, she would lose the chance to make the team for another week.

She used the tiny mirror on her desk to quickly smooth her long braided hair back with a comb. At ten years old, she was taller than most of the boys outside, but that was the least of her problems today. She decided to wear a baseball cap to hide her long hair, a sure sign that she was too female for the rest of the players. She bounded out of her room, down the stairs and past the kitchen, hoping to avoid her mother. Too late!

"Nida! Where do you think you're going in such a hurry?" It was a demand more than a question. Her mother stood near the front door, arms on her hips, irritation evident in her voice.

"I'm just going outside for a few minutes, Ma," pleaded Nida. "They'll start the game without me if I don't hurry."

Ma sighed. "You haven't even eaten breakfast yet, girl! Why do we have to go through this every weekend? You know those boys will never let you play. Why do you even bother?"

Without answering, Nida backtracked into the kitchen. She returned a minute later holding a slice of toast triumphantly. "See, here's my breakfast," she told Ma, waving the toast in the air. "I'm going out on the street for a little while, I'll be back later. Don't worry about me!"

She ran outside, ignoring the string of protests from her exasperated mother. The street seemed clean, as if someone had swept it the night before or early in the morning. Maybe one of the sweepers had come by while she was sleeping to rid the street of litter and ready it for the children to use as their personal playground all weekend. Nida savored the crisp Islamabad air, full of fragrance from the eucalyptus and mangrove trees lining the modest town homes on either side. Like many other small neighborhood streets all across the country, her street did not officially have a name, preferring anonymity to shield its families from the more exclusive atmosphere of other, named, neighborhoods. Nida's neighbors consisted of a variety of government staff, from her own schoolteacher mother to airport workers, museum and embassy staff, and many more. But, unlike those living in better neighborhoods, they comprised the lowest strata of government staff. They resided in smaller homes, struggled to make ends meet, and enjoyed the simple pleasures of life.

For Nida and many of the other neighborhood children, sport was always the best of those simple pleasures. It gave them something to look forward to, a poor man's hobby that didn't require expensive purchases or intellectual abilities. She looked around at her modest street, paved quite evenly with hardly any ruts or speed breakers, and beamed with anticipation. It was a bright spring morning, perfect for a game of cricket. Their street was a cul-de-sac, begging for children from the surrounding houses to come out and play. Yet, in Nida's neighborhood, only one sport was king. Only one sport was deemed worthy of being played on weekends: cricket.

Nida was an athletic girl, but cricket was her favorite for many reasons. She wasn't the only one; it seemed as if the entire country was in love with the sport, played on the national level by demi-gods worshipped by tens of millions of Pakistanis regardless of socio-economic class or religion. When Pakistan played a cricket match, roads and shopping centers became deserted, students were absent from school, and cafés were crowded with fans peering over each other's shoulders to watch each action replay.

On Nida's street, as in countless other streets in virtually every city, weekend mornings were reserved for cricket matches. The teams were aligned early Saturday morning and consisted of boys ranging anywhere from eight to twelve years of age. Each Saturday morning Nida would come outside hoping to be selected on one of the teams. She wasn't the only girl living on that street, but she was the lone, aspiring cricket star. It went without saying that her dreams of making the street team, despite her gender, were not taken seriously. The response of the boys on the street ranged from insensitivity to ridicule.

Nida was an optimistic and good natured ten-year-old, and she was not the least bit deterred by the seemingly hopeless situation. Her passion for cricket was hereditary, with her father and grandfather being zealous cricket fans who watched every one-day game and even the three and five-day test matches on their small television screen as if they could will the Pakistani team to victory. Then, last year, her grandfather had died and *Baba* had accepted an engineering job in Sharjah to earn a better living for his family. Left alone with her mother, an overworked secondary school teacher, Nida's only link to the father she missed terribly was his cricket fever. She wanted desperately to play. She knew she would be good because she practiced incessantly in her tiny back yard. Unfortunately, she had so far been unsuccessful in convincing the boys on her street to let her play with them.

As she stood outside her house and surveyed the birth of a new weekend game, she smiled bravely to show that she wasn't scared at the prospect of approaching the boys again. They were only boys, for God's sake, she told herself, some even younger than herself. She waved pointedly to twelve year-old Amman, the oldest one present and the self-appointed leader of the neighborhood gang.

"What do you want, Nida?" Amman called out rudely. The other boys snickered. This was their weekly routine and they enjoyed it immensely.

Nida smiled nicely. Her grandfather had used to say that it was easier to catch flies with honey than with vinegar. "You know why I'm here, Amman. Please let me play with you today." She didn't think he had experienced a change of heart or a transformation in personality in the course of a week, but it never hurt to establish boundaries early in the weekend.

He turned away from her, signaling his boredom with the conversation. "No way. You're a girl. We're not going to let a girl play cricket with us."

"Why not?" Nida addressed the second oldest, Jafar. He was the same age as Nida and a former friend. She hoped he would be more friendly and understanding of her plight. "Come on Jafar, you know I'm a good player. Please, pretty please?"

Jafar averted his eyes. Their mothers were good friends, and he had often played with Nida when they were both younger. "Sorry Nida. You know the rules. Only boys can play cricket."

"Why? Who made that rule?" She delivered that line with an impish grin that made him slightly uncomfortable.

"I don't know. It's just a rule. We can't change the rules. Don't you watch cricket on television? They don't let girls play, so why should we?" Jafar thought this was excellent logic, and all the boys apparently agreed. Nobody messed with the rules on television.

Nida wasn't so easily swayed. "Did you ever wonder who made those rules?" She challenged the statement the same way she challenged conventional wisdom in her science class at school. She was more precocious and intelligent than all these boys combined, but not mature enough, yet, to understand society's often unfair norms. Nida's mother liked to say that she only wanted to play cricket to test people's limits.

The boys obviously didn't think that rules needed assessment or analysis. "Why do you want to play, anyway, Nida?" This time the taunt came from Naveed, the youngest of the neighborhood children. "Why don't you go play with your dolls or something, like all the other girls?"

Nida glared at Naveed, who, with three sisters, probably knew more about dolls than she did. But she decided not to respond to what she knew was a cheap gibe. She turned on her heels and walked away, laughter following her. Thankfully, no one saw the tears prickling her eyes. She didn't want to give them another reason to call her a girl.

She sat down on the steps outside her house and slowly munched her toast. She needed a new strategy, she contemplated, as she ate. She had been trying to convince the boys for eight months now, ever since Baba had gone to Sharjah and left a hole in her heart. But her powers of persuasion weren't working the way she had supposed they would. She recalled her engineer father's words during his last phone call earlier in the week. "You have to think outside the box, *beti*," he had advised his daughter, amused by her descriptions of the neighborhood cricket tussle each weekend. "If one way of doing something isn't working, and you've worked hard enough at it, then you need to rethink your strategy. Find another way of solving the problem."

Hmm, what other way could there be to play cricket? Nida weighed her options. There weren't enough girls on the street to form an all-girls team. Even if she could get a number of friends together, most of them wouldn't be interested in playing cricket. She had not met any other girl her age – or any age, for that matter – who wanted to run around with a bat and get sweaty. No, if she wanted to play cricket, she had to join the boys. The only way she knew was to somehow, nicely, force them to accept her into the team. But how exactly could she accomplish that? It was obvious they weren't going to let her play out of the goodness of their hearts. They needed to be coerced somehow, but in a way that wouldn't spoil the game.

Nida was deep in thought when she spied a figure waving frantically at her from the upper story of the house opposite her own. She got up and crossed the street to the aging brown brick building – Amman's house. "What's the matter, Haleema?" she called out, hoping the girl didn't want to play. Haleema was Amman's twin sister whose favorite past-time was 'pretend salon', thanks to a new set of nail polishes sent by her aunt in Singapore.

Even if Nida had been interested in such girly games, her nails were bitten raw and in no shape to be painted.

"You're really good at math, aren't you, Nida?" The question was completely unexpected, and Nida could only nod in response. "I have a big exam coming up on Monday, and I can't understand anything in my book. If I don't pass the exam my teacher says I'll have to repeat the class. My parents are really angry. Can you help me? Please?"

Nida was slightly confused at Haleema's desperation. "What're you talking about? How can she make you repeat the class if you fail one exam?"

Haleema grimaced, her smooth brown skin crinkling at the corners of her eyes, which seemed to glitter with some sort of eye shadow. "Actually I've failed this exam three times already. She's giving me a last chance to make it up. Please, Nida? You're so good at studies, can you please help me?"

Nida would have refused, but Haleema's pleading sounded identical to her own requests for cricket. She sighed. "Okay, open the door. I can come over for a few minutes."

The minutes turned into hours, and it was noon before Nida was able to escape Haleema's house. She left with a promise to come back the next day to revise the math problems one last time. As she exited, Amman's mother called out to her from the kitchen. "Nida, *beti*, were you helping Haleema study?"

"Yes, Aunty," Nida hoped her involvement wouldn't get her in trouble, but she needn't have worried. The heavyset woman, smelling of spices and curry, came out to give her a hug that crushed her bones.

"Thank you Nida, you're a life saver! Haleema was having so much trouble in school, we were really concerned. But I'm sure, now that you've coached her, she'll easily pass the exam on Monday."

"I sure hope so," murmured Nida, anxious to leave. It was almost lunchtime and Ma would definitely be on the warpath looking for her. She waved and went out the front door. The cricket game was ending, more than ten boys now present for the final over. Nida watched enviously as Amman bowled a rocky in-swing. Abdullah, an eleven-year-old batsman who lived two houses away from her, swung wildly and hit the wickets instead. The crowd howled with laughter. Nida couldn't resist a gleeful smile. She knew she could bat much better than Abdullah, and bowl faster than Amman could. But it seemed as if she may never get a chance to show off her skills.

Amman saw her coming out of his house and scowled. She ignored his dark look and quickly crossed the street away from the action of the game and into her house. It was quiet inside. She peeked in the rooms and found Ma taking a nap on the living room sofa. Ah, peace! She found freshly cooked chicken *biryani* in the kitchen and fixed herself a plateful to take up to her room. An only child, Nida was used to doing things for herself. In fact, her independent nature demanded it and her busy mother appreciated it. The fact that she was good at her school work was an added bonus that allowed Ma to turn a blind eye to her daughter's more boisterous pursuits, such as cricket.

In her room, Nida ate the spicy rice quickly, then licked her fingers clean and settled down on her bed with her Nintendo. A gift from *Baba*, it was second-hand, but no less beloved both for the vicarious pleasure of game play as well as for the tenuous connection she felt to him each time she picked it up. She liked to imagine him dressed in his best suit, going to a fancy Sharjah store and choosing the pink device especially for her. She didn't fully understand why he had needed to leave them for a job, but she was patient by nature and preferred to miss him in secret. He called every other night, and had promised to send her a plane ticket to visit him during summer vacation. She glanced at the dog-eared calendar hanging on the wall. There were still several months before that dream would become reality.

Waving away her gloomy thoughts, Nida inserted a sports pack into the Nintendo and began to play, first squash and then golf. Since this pack contained no cricket games she had to make do with lesser sports. She had just completed the second level of golf when Ma called from downstairs. "Nida, where are you? I need something from the corner shop!"

Nida reluctantly rose from her bed with a groan and went downstairs. She knew there was no point in complaining, so she grabbed the list and money from her mother's outstretched hand and dragged her feet outside. Rafi's Corner Shop was situated at the far end of the street, merely a few minutes' walk from their house, but she preferred to take her bike so that carrying her small load of goods back would be easier. Plus, she loved riding the bike. She loved the wind blowing on her face and the feeling of utter freedom in her heart even though she wasn't allowed to leave the street.

The bicycle was another gift from *Baba*, bought a couple of years ago from a used sports goods store when he had still lived in Islamabad with them. She remembered how he had taught her to ride it, running up and down the street, holding on to its back with infinite patience. She had glimpsed Haleema and a few other girls in the neighboring houses peering out their windows, amazed at seeing a girl ride a bicycle like boys. Nida was grateful that *Baba* wasn't like other fathers, that he was sensible. He encouraged his daughter's interests and didn't care about society's narrowly defined conventions about what girls could and couldn't do.

Now, she pedaled serenely with the grace of an accomplished rider, making several rounds up and down the street before finally approaching the corner shop. There was already a man standing at the counter talking in low tones with Uncle Rafi, the owner. She expected a smile from Uncle Rafi, whom she known for as long as she could remember. His shop, the only one for kilometers, was a favorite of all age groups and all the neighborhood children called him "uncle". When Nida walked in this time, however, Uncle Rafi didn't even look at her. He was engrossed in his conversation with the man at the counter.

As Nida waited, she peered inside the shop eagerly, wondering what new toys Uncle Rafi had found to display. An extension of his small, one-story house, the shop was more like a makeshift hut on the sidewalk, its heavily angled asbestos roof defying gravity and its dark interior a source of mystery and wonder for the younger customers. Nida always loved coming here, stealing pennies from *Baba's* wallet to buy a piece of candy or a plastic toy from the shop's well-stocked cupboards. With *Baba* gone, Nida's penchant for cheap store items was mostly denied by Ma, who kept a strict eye on her purse. But today, as a reward for getting the groceries, Ma had given ten rupees to Nida to buy whatever she wanted. Only a ten year old could view a ten rupee note with such happiness. She could hardly decide what to buy.

The man ahead of her was taking too long. Nida nudged him gently and squeezed under his arm to gaze at the candy display. Caught unaware, he dropped something on the ground. He made an angry noise deep in his throat and kneeled down to look for whatever had fallen. Nida saw an open tray on the counter, filled with an array of watches. She frowned. Watches at Uncle Rafi's corner shop? They looked too expensive to be toys, and she had never before seen anything worth more than a few rupees in his shop before. What was going on here?

As if sensing Nida's inquisitive eyes on the tray, Uncle Rafi coughed and whisked away the watches. The customer straightened up, said his goodbyes and turned to leave, avoiding Nida's gaze. She didn't care, quickly dismissing the unusual scene and pouring over the candies displayed under the counter with glee. She almost forgot about Ma's list in her excitement, sheepishly handing it to Uncle Rafi at the last minute as she made her own selection. Finally, with a plastic bag full of mundane household items and a huge pink lollipop tucked into her mouth, she rode her bike back home.

* * *

Sunday dawned bright and early with the insistent ringing of Nida's alarm promptly at eight o'clock. She woke up with a start and jumped out of bed to peer out of her window. The street was empty, no sign of any neighborhood boys staking their claim yet. She heaved a sigh of relief and took her time changing clothes. For once, she felt as if this cricket challenge was getting the best of her. She had no idea how to solve the problem, and she was starting to get depressed. At her age, however, morose thoughts didn't last long. Ma yelled "Come and get your *halwa puri*, Nida!" and she bounded out of her room, spirits restored at the notion of her favorite breakfast.

Jafar's mother Tahira, the neighborhood cook, had brought the *halwa puri*. Nida was happy not just about the food, but the company as well. Tahira Aunty was a good friend of Ma's and had spent countless hours babysitting Nida in years past while Ma stayed late in school to give private lessons to the students. Tahira Aunty operated a small catering business from her home down the street, cooking delicious meals and supplying them to the local restaurants or residential customers. Today's topic of conversation, which Nida listened to with only half an ear as she munched, was a rush order of 200 *shami kabab* – beef patties. Tahira Aunty, distraught over the concept of refusing the order and losing a large amount of money, had rather hastily decided to go ahead with the task.

"I can't refuse, can I?" she asked Ma rhetorically, her glasses slipping down her nose and her hair escaping their bun as if imbued with her anxiety. "It would be like throwing money down the well, wouldn't it?" She obviously needed reassurance that she was making the right decision.

Nida's mother was, as usual, more pragmatic. "Use your common sense, Tahira. How will you make 200 *shami kabab* in one day? It's impossible."

"Not impossible," protested Tahira Aunty, the thought of all that money going to another cook hurting her in an almost physical manner. She turned to Nida in desperation. "What do you think, Nida, is it impossible to make 200 *shami kabab* in one day?"

Nida gulped her morsel and considered the matter as if her advice was being genuinely sought. "If you get some help, you should be able to do it," she finally pronounced cheerfully.

The adults had obviously not considered such a simple solution. They stared at Nida in wonder. "What a great idea, Nida!" Tahira Aunty squealed, her mood suddenly much sunnier. "Can you think of anyone who can help me at such short notice?"

Nida didn't like the way they were both looking at her. She felt herself getting hot. "Um, I don't know. Maybe you could hire somebody?"

Tahira Aunty clapped her hands. "Yes, my dear girl. What about you? Would you like to help me?"

"Me? What do I know about cooking? I'm only ten years old!" Nida was appalled that she had trapped herself into this predicament. To her, cooking *kabab* in a tiny kitchen seemed like a mindlessly boring task best performed by mothers and aunties. Then she saw Ma joining her hands together in a symbol of begging. She wants me to do this for her friend, Nida realized, and capitulated. She could hardly refuse Ma, now could she?

"Okay, I'll help you, but only if you hire me like a real helper."

Tahira Aunty beamed. "Done! I'll pay you fifty rupees in return for a day's worth of chopping and mixing."

Fifty rupees? Nida eyes grew round as she considered this turn of events. That was a colossal amount to a child her age. She could buy a lifetime's supply of lollipops with fifty rupees, maybe even the plastic train set she had seen at Uncle Rafi's shop the day before. She stood up quickly from the dining table, wolfing down the last of her *puri* and heading for the door. "Give me a couple of hours to take care of some other things, then I'll come by your house at lunch time," she called out as she left.

Ma rushed after her, grabbing her by the sleeve to stop her from leaving. "Wait, where are you going? You're not going to try to play cricket today are you?"

"No Ma, I promised Haleema I'd help her with some math. I'll be done in a little while and then I'll go to Tahira Aunty's house. Don't worry, I'm not thinking of cricket today."

Nida's mother kissed her on the cheek. "You're such a good girl, Nida. I didn't know you were helping Haleema. And now Tahira too. I'm so proud of you, my darling."

Nida didn't like all this girly emotional talk. She pushed Ma away with a grimace and ran outside before there could be any more displays of affection. She found Amman alone in the street marking the pitch for a new game. Even though she had promised her mother she wouldn't think about cricket today, she couldn't resist another plea. He was the boys' unofficial leader, and she knew she had to get through to him somehow in order to be accepted by the rest of the team. She smiled hesitantly as she approached him. "Amman, how are you?"

He didn't care for her feminine wiles. "Don't ask about the game again, Nida. It's getting tiresome." He leaned forward and scowled, a move that would have been menacing if she hadn't been taller than him. "Tell me something. Why did you go my house yesterday? Were you complaining to my parents?"

Nida was genuinely puzzled. "Complaining? About what?"

"Don't play so dumb. Why else would you go into my house? You're not friends with Haleema anymore, not since you became crazy about cricket. You must have been telling my parents about my not letting you play."

Nida was horrified that he thought she was a tattle-tale, yet slightly intrigued at the possible involvement of adults into what she had always considered a children's problem. The idea of complaining to his parents – to any of the parents – had never occurred to her. A little wheel began to turn inside her brain at his words. There was no harm in making him squirm a little bit after all the torment he had put her through. She grinned wickedly and walked away from him, towards his house. "Bye Amman, I'll see you later." She glanced back to see that his stare had wavered slightly, and she chuckled to herself. There was no need to tell him that she had a study date with Haleema.

When Nida returned to the street two hours later, the cricket game was just getting started. Wickets had been set up and Naveed was practicing googlies against a boundary wall. The boys looked up, expecting her to plead with them again, but she decided to ignore them for now. She was looking forward to earning her small fortune of fifty rupees, and she headed straight to the blue painted house towards the end of the street where Tahira Aunty lived. How hard could it be to cut up a few onions and cilantro, mix some bowls of cooked beef and lentils, and pat them into patties?

It turned out to be more laborious and time consuming than Nida could ever have imagined. When she exited Tahira Aunty's house in the evening, her fingers were cut and sore, her back was aching, and her eyes were smarting, but she was probably the richest kid on the street, perhaps even the entire neighborhood. She touched the envelope of money in her pocket to remind herself that it was real, and jogged back towards her house. She was exhausted and she could see Ma standing in the doorway waiting for her to return.

Nida was almost home when she was distracted by a loud argument nearby. The voices got louder as she approached Abdullah's house, two doors from her own. As she walked by an open window she observed Abdullah's mother and father shouting at each other. She could clearly make out the words, although she didn't understand them all because they were speaking in Punjabi, Islamabad's local language, rather than Urdu, which she understood. The topic of contention seemed to be a lost object. More than the words, she was transfixed by the expressions on the couple's faces. Her own parents had never fought in front of her, and she was lovingly shielded from the harsher aspects of their marriage, if there had been any. She slowed her pace and listened, fascinated, as they accused each other of misplacing, perhaps stealing, something very valuable. What could it be?

"Come on, Nida, hurry up! Don't loiter in the street this time of the evening!" Ma called out to her sternly, and she unwillingly walked on.

"Ma, Abdullah's mother and father were fighting," she reported as soon as she reached her mother.

"Yes I know, *beti*. It's none of our business." Ma ushered her inside and closed the front door. "They can't find a very expensive item. They came by earlier to ask if I knew anything."

Nida washed up at the kitchen sink in slow motion while Ma got dinner ready. She was drained from all that cooking and she had to go to school in the morning. "What expensive thing?" she asked almost without interest. She idly wondered what could have made Abdullah's parents so angry. If she lost something, she hardly even got punished. Perhaps because her family didn't own anything of value, she ruminated.

Ma fussed over Nida as she sat down at the table. Dinner was a simple mixed vegetable curry with homemade *chapatti*, and they both ate quietly. Ma was aware that meal times were especially difficult for Nida because she missed her father. To distract her, Ma continued to talk about Abdullah's parents as if she were telling a story.

"They had this very special watch, given to Abdullah's grandfather by the army for his thirty years of service. It was made of gold, so it was very expensive."

"A watch made of gold?" Why did that ring a bell in Nida's tired mind?

"Yes, a gold watch. Abdullah's father is convinced that his wife lost it, but she insists she didn't even touch it. It was funny in the beginning, kind of like those cartoons you sometimes watch on TV, but they are still fighting about it, so I suppose they are really angry. It must be worth a lot of money."

Nida was dozing at the table, her food half-eaten. Ma picked her up and proceeded to carry her up the stairs, not an everyday occurrence but very much deserved tonight. Nida struggled to keep her eyes open as she realized why all this talk of watches was making her uneasy. "Ma, I saw a tray of watches in Uncle Rafi's shop yesterday," she said slowly as her mother entered her bedroom and set her down on the bed.

"Rafi? Don't be silly, Nida, he doesn't sell any watches in that tiny shop." Ma closed the curtains on the window and picked up a few toys scattered across the floor.

Nida sat up. "No, Ma, I'm telling you. There was a man there, and Uncle Rafi was showing him a tray of watches, really nice golden watches. And when he saw me looking at them, he hid them. I'm telling the truth, Ma! Maybe Abdullah's grandfather's watch was in that tray." Ma pushed her back down and kissed her forehead. As she drew up a light blanket over Nida, the young girl's tired brain tried to run through all the possibilities of that statement.

Ma looked at Nida for a long minute, trying to decide if her daughter was making up the story. She knew that Nida was a very honest and intelligent little girl, not prone to daydreaming or making up stories. "Alright, Nida, I'll let Abdullah's parents know about this. They can talk to Uncle Rafi in the morning." She leaned down and kissed Nida on the forehead. "Go to sleep now, *beti*, you have school in the morning."

* * *

The week passed uneventfully for the most part. Nida pursued her usual routine of school in the morning by private van, returning home at three o'clock in the afternoon to eat lunch and then do homework until six. All the children on the street followed the same schedule, so cricket or any other extracurricular activities were strictly set aside during the week. After six o'clock she was free to play on her Nintendo or watch television. She preferred the former, allowing Ma to watch her favorite Urdu dramas in their small living room.

As she played in her room on Tuesday evening, Ma called her downstairs. Abdullah's father was at the front door, wanting to know about the watches she had seen at Uncle Rafi's corner shop. She hesitantly explained the whole story, worried that he would shout at her like he had at his wife. But he remained calm and thanked her very politely when she was finished. She went back into her room with a sigh of relief. Thankfully, she wasn't in any trouble.

Wednesday evening brought another visitor, this time Tahira Aunty, with her hair in typical disarray and her smile several watts higher than usual. "Nida, my love, your help on Sunday was invaluable!" She gushed as she sat sipping tea in their living room.

"The customer who ordered the 200 *shami kabab* was so impressed with our prompt service that she called me back today asking for more."

Nida wasn't too happy with this piece of news. "I can't make any more *kabab* with you, Aunty!" she stammered, her heart beating fearfully at the prospect of another day hunched over kitchen utensils and fresh meat.

Tahira Aunty laughed gaily. "No need, she's given me plenty of time for this order, so I can take care of it myself." She paused to take another sip of tea. "The best news is that she wants me to cook for her regularly. She's a rich lady, the wife of a diplomat, I think. She told me that she often organizes parties for her husband's work and she needs a regular caterer. She's going to give me the chance to cook for a party next weekend and prove myself."

Nida remained perplexed as Ma and Tahira Aunty erupted into excited conversation. What was the good news about lots more cooking? She decided that adults get excited about the strangest things, and left the room quietly to read a book before bedtime.

On Friday, Abdullah's father returned with some news as well. He had gone to Uncle Rafi's shop with a policeman the day before and found the tray of stolen watches Nida had described. Rafi had been hauled off to jail and Abdullah's family heritage was safely recovered, along with several other people's expensive items. Ma was suitably impressed by this efficient police action.

Nida, on the other hand, was aghast. If the police had captured Uncle Rafi, what would happen to all the candies and toys in his store? She began to tear up at this injustice. Abdullah's father, a tall man with a cropped beard that reminded her of *Baba*, noticed immediately. He kneeled down to her eye level, took her by the hand and stared at her solemnly.

"Hey, Nida, don't you worry. The shop will still be there. Rafi's brother will keep it open because everyone in the neighborhood depends on it." He smiled slightly, making his appearance much kinder. "Do you know that to me, you are a hero?"

Nida's mouth fell open. "A hero? Isn't that something only a boy can be?"

Abdullah's father smiled again. He was really quite handsome when he wasn't shouting, and she suddenly ached for her own father. "Anybody can be a hero. You did a wonderful thing by telling me about what you saw at the shop. It was very clever of you to remember. Your quick thinking and responsible behavior saved a very precious thing for me and my family. Anytime you need me or my wife to do anything for you, just let me know, okay?"

Nida nodded, her father momentarily forgotten as the wheels in her brain starting to turn once again. It was quite interesting to have a man like Abdullah's father indebted to her. He seemed very honest and trustworthy, just like *Baba*. She was already forming a plan in her devious mind, but she needed to think it through before doing anything further. "You're welcome, Uncle. I'll remember that. Thank you."

● ● ●

The rest of the week passed by quickly, and before Nida knew it, Saturday was back with its promise of cricket. But the plan she was hatching in her mind was slowly taking shape, and, for once, she wasn't going to spend her weekend running after the boys. She had finally taken her father's advice and changed her strategy. This morning, she had a strong feeling in her heart that this new approach would work.

After breakfast, she headed over to Haleema's house. The sun was shining brightly, a perfect Islamabad day. The cricket game was already in progress, with Naveed on the wicket waiting to bat. She could see Amman standing infield, glaring at her ferociously as she knocked and entered, probably dying to know why she had suddenly become a regular visitor to his house. Haleema was in her bedroom, listening to Taylor Swift on a tiny radio. She looked up as Nida entered, a smile opening her face into a beautiful flower.

"Nida! I'm so glad you're here! I have some great news!" Nida noticed that she wasn't wearing any makeup today. Even the dangly earrings she usually favored were absent.

"Oh yes? Did you pass your exam?"

"Yes! Yes! I not only passed, I got one hundred percent!" Haleema was jumping on the bed with happiness. "Can you believe it? I've never gotten a hundred percent in anything before! It's all because of you! You are so awesome!"

Nida shook her head, smiling broadly at Haleema's joy. "Nonsense, it's all your hard work. I just explained some concepts to you, and you did the rest all by yourself!" She hugged her former friend, genuinely glad for her achievement. "Congratulations!"

The door opened and Haleema's mother entered. "Nida, I'm so glad you're here! I'm sure Haleema already gave you the good news?"

"Yes, Aunty, she did. I'm so happy for her."

"*Beti*, I'd like to thank you by giving you some money. Your coaching was invaluable to her." Haleema's mother pressed an envelope into Nida's hand, but the young girl recoiled. Why did adults think every problem could be solved with money? Nida knew that gratitude didn't always have to come in an envelope, and this time, she needed something else.

"Aunty, please, I can't take this," she protested. "Haleema is my friend. I just helped her out, like friends would."

Haleema's mother looked at her wristwatch and made a little frustrated sound. "Okay, okay, don't get all upset! I have to go to the doctor and I'm already late. But I'll talk to your mother tonight at the one-dish party. Maybe she can convince you to take this reward." She smiled affectionately, waved to the girls and left the room. Nida spent a few minutes with Haleema admiring her marked exam paper before leaving as well.

She skipped as she went home. She had completely forgotten the party tonight: what a wonderful opportunity to put her new strategy into motion! Street sports weren't the only way the neighbors spent time together. While cricket was the entertainment of choice for boys, adults preferred to relax and chat over food and tea. Each season, the women living on the street planned a small pot luck dinner, a chance to gossip, admire each other's clothes and share the latest news. In the spring and summer when the days were long, the party was held outside on the street under a tent; in winters the cold weather forced them indoors at the home of a volunteer.

Tonight, as a nod to the beautiful weather they'd been having all month, the pot luck party was planned for the cul-de-sac right in front of Nida's house. Usually it was a huge bore to Nida, who stuck out like a sore thumb among the other children not only due to her height, but also because she didn't participate in conventional games, like pass-the-pillow. But tonight she vowed that the party was going to be different. For the first time she was looking forward to meeting all her neighbors, and more importantly their parents. She had come up with a strategy that *Baba* would be proud of.

By eight o'clock, everybody had arrived. Nida inspected the big folding table with an impressive array of food items donated by each family. Baked chicken and *naan* jostled with lighter fare like *samosas* and fruit *chaat*; noodles and rice for the youngsters; and desserts ranging from traditional rice pudding to chocolate éclairs. The adults, mostly women, were sitting on chairs they had all brought from their homes, talking and eating with equal gusto. The children were gathered around the drinks table, fawning over the cans of Coke and Sprite they hardly ever received permission to drink on other nights. A number of toddlers were running about on the grass with unsteady legs.

"Goo goo!" Nida glanced up from her reverie and found Naveed's baby brother standing unsteadily in front of her, smiling hugely as he brought a grasshopper towards his mouth. She called out "no, silly!" and hastily pulled the insect out of the baby's hand. Bereft of his snack, he started crying. With a mighty sigh, Nida picked him up and carried his plump little body to Naveed's mother, Nasreen Aunty.

"Oh, Nida, thank you so much! You're a life saver!" Nasreen Aunty gushed, grateful to have her baby safely back in her arms.

Reclining in the next seat, Tahira Aunty overheard the compliment, and chimed in with her own. "Yes, absolutely, I agree! Nida is only ten years old but she's such a wonderful girl. She's always willing to help people. She's such a role model for the other kids!"

Nida rolled her eyes. Tahira Aunty was really exaggerating too much. A day's worth of cooking did not make a role model. But her words were an excellent segue into the conversation Nida had planned to have with the adults at the party. She suddenly felt shy, not used to tooting her own horn. But too much was at stake to let shyness get in the way. She took a deep breath and launched her attack.

"Tahira Aunty, were you happy with my work last weekend?"

"Yes, of course, darling. I already told you I am so grateful!" Tonight Tahira Aunty's hair was secured neatly in a bun and her glasses had been replaced with contact lenses. Otherwise, she was the same old lovable surrogate-mother Nida knew.

Nasreen Aunty couldn't help ask the obvious question. "What did she do last weekend?"

"Oh, didn't I tell you, Nasreen?" Tahira Aunty readily supplied all the details of her new business contract. "I had to make

200 *shami kabab* in one day, and this little girl helped me all Sunday. I couldn't have done it without her! And now the same customer has given me another huge order. I am so delighted; I can't even begin to tell you. It was all because of Nida!"

Nida smiled through gritted teeth; all this heavy handed praise was making her very uncomfortable. Ma came to her rescue, pulling her into a warm embrace and sitting her down on a chair. "Yes, I'm very proud of my daughter too. That was very selfless of her," she agreed quietly. "She's been a big help to everyone in the neighborhood lately."

Abdullah's mother was sitting next to Nida and couldn't help but respond to this statement with an eager look on her heavily made-up face. "That's absolutely true! Your daughter is fantastic! The police caught the thief who stole our watch, you know. It was all due to the quick attention of this young girl. If she hadn't noticed those watches in Rafi's shop last week, we would never have recovered it."

The ladies all oohed and aahed appropriately. The discussion veered towards other incidents of theft, and the importance of insuring valuable items, until Nida worried that her cause would be forgotten. She had to get the conversation back on track, and quickly.

She looked around for Haleema and Amman's mother, who was sitting a few chairs away talking with another neighbor. Nida got up and walked over to her, pulling on her arm to get her attention. "Aunty, did you tell everyone about Haleema passing the math exam?" she prompted.

Haleema's mother looked up, a little bemused to be approached thus by a child. "Yes, thank you for reminding me, Nida." She straightened up and turned slightly to address the group. "My daughter Haleema got a hundred percent in her math exam thanks to Nida's tutoring last weekend. And I totally forgot, I wanted to give her a little reward but she refused."

She opened her purse, but Nida shook her head. "No thank you Aunty. I don't want your money."

"Don't feel offended, dear girl. I just wanted to show my gratitude." Haleema's mother looked at her askance.

"I have a better idea of how you can do that," said Nida boldly.

"What are you talking about, Nida?" Ma interjected, looking slightly embarrassed at her daughter's temerity.

Nida took a deep breath. It was now or never, she thought. "You all probably know I like playing cricket, right?"

The ladies laughed. Nida's passion was no secret to anybody on the street.

Nida continued, her courage bolstered by the adults' attention. "Your sons – Amman, Abdullah, Naveed, even Jafar – won't let me play with them. They have this silly rule about girls not being able to play cricket. But you see, aunties, how a girl like me was able to do all these things that the boys couldn't do? I helped catch a thief, and I tutored class seven math, even though I'm in class five. Oh, and I helped make 200 *kabab*! Can you believe that? Because of my help, Tahira Aunty got more business. Don't you think I could play a little cricket?"

There was silence in the camp as the women digested this little girl's daring speech. She captured their imagination in a manner that was charming and wholesome. She was a sight to behold, dressed in a maroon tunic and long grey *pajama*, hair knotted in a French braid that showed off her delicate features and promised beauty in years to come. Her words were confident, belying the turmoil in her stomach that made her clench her mother's hand tightly under the folds of Ma's *dupatta*. Her passion was obvious, and even the boys about whom she complained in such a pleasing style were drawn to the scene.

"Aunties, I didn't do all those things for money. I did it because you are all like my family. What I need in return for your gratitude is that you ask your sons to let me play with them," Nida continued in a strong little voice. "I don't want to be captain, or chase them away. I want to be their friend, to play together with them, that's all."

After a short silence, Tahira Aunty turned to the boys. "What do you think, Jafar, can she play with you? She's done a lot for us. I wouldn't have gotten that high-paying job without her."

Jafar nodded slowly. He had seen Nida practice in the afternoons, and as captain he was sure he could easily win with her on his team. But he didn't want to seem too eager, since until last weekend he had refused to consider her petition. "Yeah sure, we can let her try out. Right, Amman?"

Amman glared at this betrayal, but he was also relieved he didn't have to tutor his sister anymore. Perhaps Nida could help him with his math as well, he thought to himself. In any case there was that cool Nintendo he wanted to try out – the only one on the street. He looked carefully at Nida. "Yes, I suppose it will be okay for you to play with us. But if you get hurt you're not allowed to cry."

Nida's face broke out in the widest grin Ma had ever seen. She jumped up and down, shrieking "Thank you! Thank you!" until she ran out of breath. Ma smiled to see her daughter so exultant. It had been a while since Nida had laughed this freely, expressed such carefree happiness. Not since her father had gone to Sharjah.

That reminded her that it was getting late. Ma stood up and took Nida by the hand. "Excuse me, ladies," she said to her friends. "It's almost time for Nida's father to call. She will be so excited to tell him the good news."

Mother and daughter waved goodbye and started towards their house. Nida skipped slightly ahead, her smile still fixed to her face. Tomorrow was Sunday, a day of lazy mornings, delicious breakfasts, family visits, and most of all, cricket. But this Sunday, Nida would not be watching from her window. She would take charge of her destiny and play a real street match for the first time. Tomorrow seemed like the beginning of a new life, and for the first time in eight months she felt whole. Who knows, one day she might be the first female cricket player of her city, even her country. Who knows, by the time she grew up, the rules on television may change and girls could be allowed to have their own team, or even play with the boys. Nida sighed happily. A girl could dream, couldn't she?

Free My Soul

Freedom has a price, but only those who are truly captive understand what it is. As I write the final words in my journal today, I cannot think of anything else. For the last ten years, the price of freedom had been too high for an undeserving woman like me to pay. But today it seems like a paltry sum. How can such an upheaval in personal philosophies have occurred? As I prepare to leave one stage and enter another, anxiety mixes with exhilaration to form an unfamiliar emotional blend. Why should I worry now, when the fears of the past decade have finally come to an end in such an unconventional way? In effect, this journey from captivity to freedom and then back into another type of captivity is my entire story, but to tell it I have to start at the beginning and then come back to the end – to today.

My name is Lubna and I am thirty-one years old. You who are reading this may find it interesting that after everything I have been through, these few words and numbers are all I can say about myself, as if I am a student introducing myself to the class for the first time. I do this perhaps because I feel safe in the anonymity that this brief profile affords me. After all, people cannot judge me if they know nothing about me other than my name and my age. Yet, putting a number on my life makes me strangely uncomfortable, as if in my mind I still yearn for the innocent young girl I used to be.

Perhaps I should write that sentence again: My name is Lubna and I am a thirty-one year old inmate at the women's section of the

Karachi jail. What a difference these few additional words make. All of a sudden I can almost see you, my reader, begin to judge, to wonder who I am and why I am in jail. What sort of criminal would write about herself as if inviting sympathy or pity? What crime did she commit? Was she innocent or guilty?

The truth is that I write not for sympathy but because of a promise made to a friend. This promise, and the journal you hold in your hand, are the reasons I still have hope in my heart today despite the misfortunes I have borne. But I know from books and magazines that a story must be told in chronological order lest the reader get confused. So with many apologies, let me start at the beginning.

I came to the women's section of the Karachi jail at the age of twenty one on a false charge of theft. Nobody, including myself, would have thought this accusation on my character would have such a transformative effect, both negative and positive, on my future and the future of those closest to me. Before the incident that changed my life, I was poor but happy; recently married and mother to a newborn son. When I look back at that time it seems hazy and silent, as if that life belonged to someone else. In a way it did, because I can say with surety that I am not that Lubna of long ago, who loved her family with passion and her employment with gusto.

I was born in a big family, the youngest of five children. We were poor and school was not only a luxury but a distraction as well, taking healthy bodies away from work. My parents were devout Muslims and they taught me Arabic so that I could pray. When I turned six they sent me for daily studies at the local mosque to learn to recite the Quran. I have heard of uneducated and abusive Imams teaching by rote, but thankfully mine was a good man. He not only taught his students how to read Arabic but also explained the meanings of the words we were reading. This meant that despite the poverty keeping my parents so exhausted, I was able to learn the basics of my religion and attain the important concepts of peace, justice, charity, forgiveness and prayer. For these early lessons that have lasted a lifetime, I am eternally grateful. I couldn't have survived the catastrophes in my life without them.

My mother was the nanny at a wealthy businessman's house; we called him *Sahib Ji* out of respect. My father was the gardener at the same mansion, although he worked odd jobs at various other homes as well. *Sahib Ji's* wife was a socialite, spending many mornings shopping and evenings partying, but as all rich Pakistani women she still commanded her household. My parents were only two of the half dozen or so servants who worked day and night for *Sahib Ji*. Such is the nature of economic life in our country, that the rich and the poor simultaneously depend on each other – one for an honest living, the other for the maintenance of a certain lifestyle.

My older siblings stayed with my aunt while my mother worked, but as the youngest I couldn't bear to be separated from my mother for long periods of time. Therefore, as a child I spent a lot of time in *Sahib Ji's* kitchen and back yard, quickly becoming friends with his daughter Samreen who was close to me in age. *Sahib Ji* and his wife were happy with this arrangement, asking my mother to bring me along every day for their daughter's entertainment. Yet, my presence there wasn't idle by any means. While Samreen was at school each morning, I helped the other servants around the house, and in the process learned many skills from them: cooking delicious food from the elderly chef Salma, washing and ironing clothes from the maid Huma, and even basic carpentry skills from the driver/handyman Abdul Shakoor. I was intelligent and loved to learn anything and everything. How sad that it never occurred to anyone that given the opportunity to study, I would similarly excel at academics.

As a young girl on the lowest rung of the socio-economic ladder, I knew that the talents acquired in *Sahib Ji's* house would be of immense benefit when I started working myself. My dreams revolved, not around raising a family or gaining an education, but on finding a kind employer to hire me as a cook in his home. I had discovered that in any rich household the cook held a position of authority and usually earned more money than the other servants, and my aspirations to be in such a position motivated me to spend countless hours at Salma's side, soaking up knowledge of the most scrumptious kind.

What I didn't know was that this near-perfect existence was about to change. As I turned into a teenager, two watershed events in my life changed my dreams significantly. First, my father died of pneumonia when I was fifteen, catching a cold during an unexpected rain in the winter season. His loss meant more to our family in terms of lost income than the absence of a parent. My two older brothers, nineteen and eighteen respectively, had already been working part-time in a mechanic's shop. After my father's death, they became full-time workers intent on scraping enough together to feed the family. My mother, who had transitioned from nanny to housekeeper at *Sahib Ji's* house as Samreen grew older, actively started searching for suitors for my third and fourth siblings, my sisters Amina and Uzma, whose marriages would mean two less mouths to feed. I watched with anxious eyes the changes taking place in my humble home, wanting to go back in time to my childhood, where I was content despite the poverty.

Three years passed and slowly the uncertainty dissipated for the time being. The second event that drastically affected my life was the arrival of Samreen's maternal uncle Waseem at *Sahib Ji's* house when I was sixteen. My dear reader, even writing the hated name on this paper makes me nauseous. Waseem had been working as a police inspector in Hyderabad, a city less than 150 kilometers from Karachi. For reasons unknown to me, he left his job and moved into *Sahib Ji's* house. At approximately the same time I was hired as the aging cook Salma's assistant. My employment was a boon to my family. With my two older brothers now working full-time, two sisters somewhat happily married, and my own new status as heir to the kitchen throne at *Sahib Ji's*, it was easy for my mother to finally retire. I was close to achieving my dreams, unsuspecting of the future.

The Quran says that Allah is the best of planners. While I witnessed His planning at later stages of my life, it seemed that in my youth it was other human beings who were making plans on my behalf. With ample time on her hands now that she had retired, my mother began planning my matrimonial future. The matchmaking lady in our neighborhood started arriving daily in my absence to show her photographs of prospective grooms and she would pressure me to marry one of these poor souls as soon as I entered the door late at night. I didn't have any qualms about getting married, even if the match was arranged, as is our custom – after all, marriage is as much a part of our lives as work. But after a hard day of slicing several pounds of onions and potatoes, making a variety of colorful salads, cooking perfectly rounded *chapattis*, scrubbing tons of pots and pans and finally cleaning the huge kitchen until it gleamed for the next day, I had no desire to listen to my mother's lectures and decide which young man would be the best husband. I was sixteen, financially independent, and feeling on top of the word. What use did I have for a husband?

For the next three years, I dedicated myself to become the best cook I could possibly be, whipping up a delicious array of appetizers, entrées and desserts to please my master and mistress, as well as Salma, my supervisor. Not only would I pester Salma for the best cooking techniques, but in my quest for perfection I would seek recipes from television shows and even knock on the neighbors' doors on my day off, asking for secret family recipes. My hope was that after Salma retired, which seemed imminent due to her advancing age and weakening eyesight, I would be selected to take her place in the kitchen. Even if things did not go according to plan and another cook was hired, I thought, I could always count on *Sahib Ji*, his wife and my childhood playmate Samreen to give me glowing references. I had no doubt that my dedication and long years of service had endeared me to them and would ultimately result in a significant improvement of my economic status.

This strategy may have been successful were it not for the secret plans of another person in the household, Waseem. He was at least fifteen years older than me, physically unattractive and spiritually dead. Although I never spoke more than two words at a time to him in all the years I worked at *Sahib Ji's* house, I gained terrible insight into his character just by observing him and his activities. He was lazy and rude, not caring about anybody but himself. I had grown up in *Sahib Ji's* house, where owners and servants alike were polite and respectful. To me, Waseem was a shocking new representation of the country's privileged elite. He was rumored to be wealthy, yet he was living in his sister's home as if he needed the assistance. In the eyes of a hardworking person like me, this was unacceptable.

His activities made him even more unappealing. He would wake up at noon, spend the day watching television or talking on the phone, and when night fell, a steady stream of friends bearing drugs, alcohol and playing cards would descend on the house. Practicing Muslim that I was, these habits seemed disgusting to me; I could not understand how they could be tolerated by the owners of the house. I would usually be leaving just as his friends would start to arrive, so I missed the revelry that poor *Sahib Ji* and his wife must have been subjected to all those years. It was a testament to the kind nature of this couple that they would allow Waseem to take such advantage of these circumstances.

That Waseem was a corrupt, godless individual came as no surprise to me. I decided that it was none of my business how he spent his days and nights, and therefore tried my best to avoid him. But, as is the nature of human corruption, Waseem inevitably set his impure eyes on me. For three years, he attempted to get close to me even as I shied away. He would try to touch me as I passed by, ogle me with lewd eyes, whisper offensive proposals in my presence. Having been raised in a devout household and fully cognizant of my religious teachings, I did not feel at all flattered by his attention. While I had seen maids in other households succumb to the charms of their bored masters, I was under no false hope that Waseem would make me his Cinderella. My voracious appetite for Pakistani and Indian movies seen on the tiny television screen in *Sahib Ji's* servant quarters during the afternoon hours meant that I fully understood the social inequities between us.

What Waseem desired from me and what I needed in a man were two very different realities, and I was absolutely not interested in a sordid romance that would soil not only my chastity but also my reputation as a cook. So every time I met him in the house or outside, I gathered my wide *chador* around my head and body, lowered my gaze and passed by him without a sound. In our highly religious culture, such a wordless exchange of request and refusal were thankfully sufficient. After a few months of suggestive glances and inappropriate catcalls in my presence, Waseem got the message.

My unavailability was further cemented in his mind when at the age of nineteen I married one of the many suitors clamoring for my hand. My new husband's name was Shahid; he was a kind and gentle young man only a year older than I was and he made a decent living as a taxi driver. Even more importantly he was literate, having studied until tenth grade. His education was a huge factor in my decision; it meant that we could together dream of leaving behind the poverty we both grew up in by working hard and seeking employment of a different kind than manual labor. My mother, wise woman that she was, knew, however, that work alone does not make a happy marriage. She did an excellent job as matchmaker: our personalities and appearances matched well and we were happy. A year later my son Adil, the apple of my eye, was born, and I finally understood what unconditional love meant. He stayed in my mother's care while I worked, and I missed him every minute of every day.

While my personal and professional life seemed to be prospering with each passing year, I was unaware that my future was being written with decidedly dark ink. As I was soon to find out, Waseem was livid that I had rejected him with all his wealth and chosen a lowly taxi driver over him – never mind that the relationship he was offering was reprehensible and temporary. He deemed my standoffishness a great insult and decided to make my life a living hell – something he was uniquely qualified to do. By the time I had turned twenty one, he had conspired to hurt me beyond my wildest imaginations. Like dominos marked with the hand of fate, my world collapsed around me all because of one man.

One day in summer as I mixed cake batter for the evening's dessert, *Sahib Ji's* wife strode into the kitchen with a look of great consternation on her face. I stood uncomprehending as she accused me in a shrill tone of stealing some jewelry. At first I didn't take the accusation seriously. In a household that size, items routinely went missing, and owners typically held servants responsible. I promised to look for the jewelry as soon as I finished cooking, thinking the issue would resolve itself before the day ended. Her anger increased along with the volume of her voice, and soon all the servants were gathered around gawking at this unusual display of fiery emotions from a normally temperate personality. After some time I ascertained that the lost item was extremely valuable in terms of both monetary and sentimental value – a diamond necklace handed down through generations from mother to daughter and destined for Samreen's graceful neck on her upcoming wedding next year.

When I heard the word diamonds, I finally understood the enormity of the situation I was in. The more I protested my innocence, the louder my mistress screamed. She insisted she had a witness, and I wondered who it could be when there had been nothing to witness. Finally she divulged that Waseem had claimed to see me enter her bedroom the day before and quietly leave a few minutes later with a package wrapped in cloth. I was horrified. It goes without saying, dear reader, that I did not steal that necklace. If my Islamic upbringing full of honesty and principles was not sufficient to keep me from doing so, then my disposition towards hard work to improve my lot in life should convince you that I was not a thief. Sadly, even though all of *Sahib Ji's* household, owners and servants combined, had known me my entire life, they assumed the worst and labeled me as such.

I continued to deny it, of course, and finally invited her to search my belongings. She grimly informed me that the police had been alerted, because Waseem was sure that I had taken the necklace home with me the night before. I spent the rest of the day filled with dread; the word, "police", had injected an immense sense of worry and doom into my typically carefree mind. Our police are notoriously dishonest and inefficient, easily bought and sold to the highest bidder. I had watched countless reality television shows profiling the ineptitude and corruption of the police, and had often seen officers in our neighborhood harassing the residents in exchange for favors. That this description was a stereotype did not occur to me until later, when I met police officers of a very different nature. For the time being, Waseem, a former policeman from

Hyderabad himself, seemed the embodiment of a corrupt police culture, and I became thoroughly scared.

By that evening, things had progressed into a full-scale catastrophe. Two constables arrived at *Sahib Ji's* house with a package in their hand. To my horror, the diamond necklace had been discovered in my house, and there was nothing I could say to deny this impossible fact. My guilt was proven without my having to lift a finger, and in a fit of rare anger I screamed that if I had wanted to steal the necklace surely I would have hidden it in a less obvious place. But nobody was listening. For reasons I cannot decipher, poor people are always assumed stupid, as if intelligence comes only from heavy books and expensive schools.

Sahib Ji had come home from his business by then. When he was apprised of the situation, the man looked positively betrayed. I wanted to plead to him, but it was obvious from his expression that he was devastated and would not listen. He had known my parents for decades and I had practically grown up under his care. In all those years nothing like this had ever happened, but instead of being assured of my innocence, this seemed to cement his belief in my guilt. I often think that wealthy people suspect everyone poor of bad intentions just waiting to be exposed – as if religion, principles or morals count for absolutely nothing when confronted with a sack of money or a jewel-encrusted necklace. All those years of honest work guarding *Sahib Ji's* children and his valuables in his absence, the trust put in my mother and then in me, came crashing down with the ugly act of a relative. Waseem had won. I had lost.

With dizzying rapidity, I was handcuffed roughly by the constables and hauled into the police van outside. As I left, I looked back to see Waseem almost smirking in satisfaction. An intense hate filled my chest, and I vowed to prove my innocence if it took my entire life. Today, I laugh painfully as I write these words. Although my intentions at that time were pure, I had no idea what was about to happen. Growing up poor should have illustrated to me the realities of deprivation and injustice, but somehow my loving parents had protected me from everything negative until that fateful day. Their affection and work ethics had enveloped me while I grew up, and *Sahib Ji's* good nature and expansive home provided a safe haven for me all those years. I had never understood the ugliness in other people's nature because I had not seen it reflected in those closest to me.

I was about to receive an education like no other. Now that I look back at that time in my life, I realize how naïve I was to expect a political and legal system that would actually allow me to prove my innocence. As my expectations fell in those later years, my depression grew. But, for the moment, as I traveled to the jail in that stifling van, I was consumed with a strange mixture of fear and rage born of adrenaline alone. I was ready to fight – not only for myself but for my family's name and honor. I was well aware that word of the alleged theft would quickly circulate my neighborhood and my family would be labeled thieves by association. They would be ridiculed and suspected forevermore, thanks to this one fabrication.

I also had another pressing concern. Throughout the van ride, I agonized over the thought of being imprisoned. I remembered a local television program from several years ago; a reporter had gone undercover with a video camera to film several prisons in the two provinces of Sindh and Punjab. Feelings of horror washed over me as I recalled the long-forgotten images of cramped sleeping quarters and filthy living conditions. The rats in those jails were bigger than my shoes. The jailors had huge mustaches on their faces and long sticks in their hands. As I had watched the program I wondered who was worse: the abusive, power-drunk wardens or the hardened, violent criminals they watched over.

I realized that my indignation over being accused of theft hid not only a worry for my family but also a deeper fear of living in jail for even a short period of time. After a while I decided that there was no use worrying over something so insanely out of my control. Allah alone could be my Helper in such an impossible situation. I tried to repel all negative thoughts by silently praying every prayer my mother had ever taught me, and when I ran out of prayers I started reciting every chapter of the Quran that I had memorized over the years. My fear was immense but I somehow felt calmer as I reached the van's destination.

My prayers seemed to me to have worked in a magical way. When I embarked I found the women's section of the Karachi central jail to be very different from my imagination. It was clean, airy, and well-kept, with none of the filth and disarray I had seen in that television program long ago. The barracks were open and clean, not at all over-crowded as I had expected. The constables and wardens, all females, were polite and sympathetic. Seeing my anxiety they flocked to my side and assured me of my safety, a novel concept considering the tales of mean-spirited police officers I had heard. But, despite their caring attitude I was apprehensive. I didn't know what the future held for me; no-one had bothered to explain the legal process to me yet, or the steps I could take to attain my freedom.

Two days passed without answers. I was given a bed with fifteen other inmates in the barrack, food to eat and plenty of rest. But sleep was impossible and I ate only to distract myself from my ever-increasing worry. That the jail was satisfactory beyond my expectations was of little comfort to me. After all, a window with bars signifies captivity, even if the bars are clean and the curtains beautifully patterned. My worries shifted from myself to my husband and son. What was Shahid thinking of my disappearance? How was my one-year-old Adil coping without me? Did my family think I really stole that necklace? And finally, why had Waseem done what he had?

The last question was easy to answer once I thought about it: revenge. Waseem was of the class of human beings better known as animals. He had been furious at my tacit refusal of his depraved proposal, and he had sought revenge in the worst possible way. I feared that my own punishment would spill over to my innocent family, but I was unaware to the extent that it had already done its damage. A visit on the third day of my imprisonment shocked me to my core.

Three days after I arrived at the jail, I was visited by a volunteer lawyer who had been assigned by the state because I could not afford one. This, in itself, astounded me, and I am sure must be unbelievable to some Pakistanis used to the uncaring attitude of the state. The truth is that my jail was atypical in many respects. Volunteer lawyers were one of the many ways the women's jail assisted inmates. The counsel was not highly experienced, but at least it was free. I counted my blessings when Hina arrived. She told me that she was a final year law student and I was her eleventh case. Working under the auspices of a barrister, two of her prior cases had been resolved, and five, including mine, were pending. I took it as a positive sign, although I didn't really have any choice in the matter.

Hina gave me an update on my case, much of which was devastating news to me. My husband Shahid had been arrested as an accomplice when the police had searched my house. He was at the men's section of the central jail awaiting a lawyer. My son Adil was with my mother, but her situation too was dire since our landlord had evicted her to disassociate himself with my alleged crimes. She was staying with my sister Amina whose in-laws had also threatened to turn her out. I finally understood the enormity of Waseem's actions, and for a cursed moment, regretted ever denying him what he had wanted from me. How could all this have happened in the blink of an eye? Could the repayment for sticking to one's morals really be so painful?

Thankfully, Hina believed that I was innocent. As I continued to discover during my stay at the women's jail, a large number of inmates had been framed by jealous relatives, spurned lovers or even complete strangers looking to make money off of someone else's misery. But despite my innocence, Hina had no hopes of the quick dismissal of my case. She reminded me that a rich and powerful man was behind the accusation, and legal judgments typically followed the rule that might was right. She advised me to expect delays in my case, and to worry exclusively about my son at that moment.

She was right, of course. My insides were gnawing with anguish at the thought of Adil crying for me. Hina told me that children could remain in the jail with their mothers until the age of seven, and she would start the process to have Adil come live with me as soon as possible. She also promised to find out what she could about Shahid's fate. I cringed when I thought how much he must hate me. Not as much as I hated myself at this point.

Time passed excruciatingly slowly. My mother brought Adil to meet me every week, and I didn't have the heart to tell her that his anguished cries, as they left each time, were too much for me to bear. I often wished that I couldn't see him anymore, then immediately felt horrible for thinking such a thing about my own child. Thankfully, the repeated separations didn't last long and Adil finally received permission to come live at the jail five months after my imprisonment began. At the same time my mother's health began to rapidly deteriorate. She succumbed to the stress of being ostracized by her family and friends, dying of a stroke one year later. I wondered at the cruel hand of fate, which had reunited me with my son with one hand, and snatched away the life of my mother with the other. If Allah had a plan for me, I was unable to perceive it.

My case dragged on. Each court appearance would take an entire day, beginning with optimism and ending in despair. Due in part to Waseem's influence with the police and in part to the ineptitude of the legal system itself, each hearing was subsequently postponed to another date months later. Sometimes the delay occurred due to city-wide strikes that would close offices and restrict traffic in protest of political or religious events. Strikes are a frequent occurrence in Karachi, but never before had I understood the detriment they have on so many. At other times the delay would be a result of another lawyer's absence. Since my case was tied to Shahid's, both our lawyers had to be present together before the judge. If either was unable to appear the case was delayed.

My husband was a continuing source of anxiety to me in those days. I had not seen him since the day of my arrest. In the months that followed I had accompanied Hina to the courts several times, but he was not present even once. I longed to lay my eyes on his beloved face, to assure him of my innocence, to beg forgiveness for unwittingly putting him in such a desperate situation. Finally after numerous inquiries I was told that he had contracted typhoid soon after his arrest and was severely ill. My fear for his health strengthened my connection to Allah, and I began to pray for him constantly. According to Hina his prison was one of the most notorious for jailer abuses. Not surprisingly, in his weakened state he was unable to recover and continued to suffer mentally and physically for a long time. Finally, two years after he first entered the jail, Shahid died without ever having his day in court.

I remember vividly the day I became a widow. It was spring. The day was beautiful even for Karachi. I was sitting outside in the jail's garden watching Adil play among the flowers. Yes, dear reader, it may come as a surprise but the jail has a garden, full of tall trees and all kinds of plants whose names I am not familiar with. Nobody knows if the garden is an oasis for the wardens or therapy for the inmates, but everybody enjoys it equally during the mild weather. Hina entered the hushed space in haste, her presence itself told me that something was wrong. She was not scheduled to meet me for another three weeks. I got up from my seat to confront her, knowing intuitively that it would be bad news but wanting to hear it nonetheless. She told me with tears in her eyes that Shahid had passed away in the prison infirmary the night before and that his lawyer had personally called to tell her that morning.

As I sank to the ground in grief, I experienced a myriad of emotions swirl in my breast. On one hand, the bitterness of my dear husband's death in the prime of his life was a huge blow. At the same time, though, I felt relieved that the pain of his illness and the indignity of the prison abuses he had been facing were finally over. Hina sat down on the ground with me and hugged me for long minutes. I clung to the knowledge that even in jail I was not completely alone, that my husband's death had an impact on this kind girl, as well. In the last two years she had become much more than a volunteer honing her legal skills. She had become my confidante, my friend, even my therapist.

A few weeks afterwards, I received my first and only letter. How ironic that while alive, Shahid and I had not been allowed to communicate with each other, yet he could almost reach out from the grave to touch me. He had written the letter in his last few days, with instructions to his lawyer to deliver it to me after he died. The letter had traveled through innumerable twists and turns in the complicated legal system before reaching me, and provided a beacon of hope in my sadness. Hina read it to me, apologizing every few minutes for the necessary invasion of privacy. Aside from a characteristic declaration of love, Shahid absolved me from any guilt in the tragedy of the last two years.

Shahid's letter was more precious to me than any other possession. The courts may find me guilty one day, but Shahid had died believing in my innocence, and to me that was all that mattered. Still, the case was important for a number of reasons, and hope was dwindling daily. It took another two years for the judge to pronounce what he had probably decided from the beginning: that I was indeed a thief. Waseem was sitting in the courtroom the day my sentence was given, in the same place he had occupied at every hearing for the past four years. He stared at me with a hard expression as I was awarded seven years for theft. I suppose I should have railed at the injustice of being presumed guilty by a system set up on the shaky foundations of bribery and nepotism, rather than fair play and evidence. But my morale was lower than the ground I walked on, and I was relieved that the sentence wasn't any greater.

After the verdict, Hina explained to me that, as I had already spent four years in jail, I would now only be required to complete the remaining three years before I would be free. I could hardly believe it! Three years seemed virtually painless for someone who had already spent more time than that behind bars. I considered it an immense blessing that least Adil and I were together, that my misfortunes had not greatly affected my son at such a tender age. Hopefully he would not even remember these few years in imprisonment when he was older. You may find it difficult to believe, reader, but the truth was that the jail was a haven not just for me but all the wretched inmates – a refuge for our miserable existences that would have been paradise in any other situation. Many of the women living there came from such poor backgrounds that the jail was actually an improvement. I suspect I was the only one missing my busy days, my work as a cook.

I decided to take this as an opportunity to spend time with my son in a way that my parents had never been able to do with me or my siblings. Apart from myself, five of the inmates in my barrack had children staying with them. One had three children under the age of seven. We could have tried to bond for the sake of our children but life had dealt each of us a bad hand and we no longer trusted anyone. The children played together constantly, but the mothers were usually much more reserved and skeptical. It goes without saying that living in such close proximity often resulted in complicated relationships between the inmates. The wardens tried to keep the peace but sometimes personalities clashed and groups formed. I remained on the outskirts of these relationships, but sometimes I was drawn in despite my best efforts. For instance, a row erupted between two inmates one year over the best seat in front of the barrack television set, and I was chosen as the judge to decide who would sit where. Obviously this position led to unhappiness on both sides, with me caught in the middle.

A year after that, petty arguments between some children in the barrack led their mothers to abandon prior friendships and develop new enmities. Adil and I tried to remain neutral but it cost him a good friend. In any case, I quickly became known as the quiet one who could usually not be influenced in a conflict. To keep myself busy and away from inmate politics, I asked the jail administration if I could do something. They were probably surprised but gave me kitchen duties, which I thoroughly enjoyed.

My son Adil, meanwhile, was growing rapidly, oblivious to the strangeness of his surroundings. When he was born, I had promised myself that I would send him to school so that he would have more opportunities in life than I did, or my parents. His future was still uppermost in my mind now that I was imprisoned, so when he turned three I enrolled him in the jail Montessori. Yes, dear reader, you read that right. The jail did not only have a school, but a certified Montessori! It was a small room but a joy nonetheless, filled with color and imagination. The volunteers who came to teach were very understanding of the trauma the children had been through, for which I was grateful. He blossomed under their care, becoming the little boy I am sure Shahid would have been proud of.

My kitchen duties in the jail were minimal, and, not used to having so much free time on my hands, I too decided to fulfil a dream of mine. At the age of twenty five, the same year as my verdict, I joined the adult literacy class in the jail and became a student along with my young son. Volunteers of different types frequented the jail, and I persuaded one to teach me other subjects, as well. My thirst for knowledge was insatiable, and Mrs. Akeel, a retired school teacher, found me to be the perfect pupil. As Adil and I learned to read and write almost simultaneously, grappled with small math problems, and recited facts of history to each other at the end of the day in lieu of bedtime stories, I felt a surge of pride at our survival, despite the odds. Little did I know that my saga was far from over.

When Adil turned seven he was no longer eligible to live in the jail with me. I asked my sister, Uzma – the only relative who still came to visit me once a year on *Eid* – if she could take him, but she refused, citing her growing family and small home. I was scheduled to be released in ten months, so with some hesitation I requested the jail to transfer Adil to the same place all inmates' children went when they turned seven: the SOS Village. Hina had told me some months earlier that SOS is a national nonprofit organization running orphanages in several countries of the world, and I agreed to allow them to safeguard my precious son until I came for him.

When the day arrived for Adil to leave, the entire jail – staff, volunteers and inmates – came out to say goodbye. There was cake and hand-made presents, a very humble going-away party in anticipation of my own release later that year. I was teary-eyed, but positive that our ordeal was about to end. I hugged and kissed him, told him to be a good boy, and let him leave, not knowing what lay in store for both of us.

When Hina rushed into the garden the next day, I thought I was dreaming of Shahid's death so many years ago. Her panic was identical to the one four years ago, and immediately I knew another nightmare was about to begin. The van taking Adil to the SOS Village had been intercepted by masked gunmen, the driver killed and my son abducted. Sadly, such crimes are common in Karachi, so the police took their time arriving to the scene and witnesses were nowhere to be found. It was only after the SOS administration was notified that they realized Adil was missing. By that time he was obviously long gone.

Hina was explaining, but I could hardly hear her over the tumultuous uproar in my heart. I felt as if the world was crashing around me. Shahid's death, even my arrest, could not compare to this loss. At the same time I was not completely surprised. I had known at least three women over the course of my lifetime whose children had been kidnapped – a next door neighbor, a distant cousin, and even Huma, the maid in *Sahib Ji's* house. I have heard that these kidnapped children are big business, the backbone of many illegal, but tolerated, industries including child prostitution and begging. With more children being born daily to replace those lost by disease, death or human actions, a child's kidnapping seems an inconsequential event until it happens to a mother, I suppose.

Upon hearing the news of Adil's abduction, I suffered a physical and mental breakdown, spending weeks in bed surviving on antidepressants provided by the staff doctor. Questions kept swirling in my mind. I wanted to scream at Allah for allowing all of the world's misfortunes to befall me. But I had no energy, no will, even for anger.

Two months after the kidnapping, when I was still mildly deranged, I was informed of a visitor. I didn't want to see anyone but I dragged myself outside to the visitation area, thinking it may be one of my siblings. Imagine my shock, dear reader, at seeing

Waseem's hateful figure on the other side of the bars. Had he come here to mock me, or threaten me? Didn't he know that nothing he could do now would surpass what had already been done to me by the cruel hand of fate? Before I could speak he held up a photograph. It took me a minute to realize that it was of Adil, wearing the second-hand striped shirt and black pants I had so lovingly helped him put on before bidding him goodbye. I looked at the picture uncomprehendingly for a while, struggling to make sense of it. Was it possible? How could it? Waseem was my son's kidnapper?

Indeed I was right. He told me that Adil was alive, even gave me the name of the neighborhood where he was keeping him. He was taunting me, wanting to make sure that when I came out of the jail in a few months, I would have nothing to live for. This, then, was the final revenge for spurning him. Some men throw acid on their beloved's faces to ruin them, Waseem had taken my lifeblood away from me. I wished fervently I had never rejected him. Anything would have been better than this torturous hell.

My health deteriorated even further and the jail warden decided to postpone my release until I was better able to take care of myself. Those days passed in a haze. I was told later that I tried to commit suicide twice – once by swallowing a bottle of cleaning liquid left in my barracks by a volunteer cleaner, another time by slashing my wrists repeatedly with a butter knife. Hina came to see me often during that time. She had graduated from law school soon after my sentence was announced and joined a small legal practice helping mostly female clients like myself. Despite her busy schedule she often made time to see me, especially when I was so ill. I remember her worried expressions and her quiet attempts to coax me out of my depression. But it was useless. I was locked into a deep trance, my ears shut to the sounds of the outside world. I stopped praying, abandoned the daily reading of the Quran, and forgot all about Allah. Or rather, began to hate Allah and His empty promises. I forgot everything but my own misery.

The jail staff was all extremely concerned for me, as Hina later recounted. Understanding that I needed time to heal, the superintendent contacted the judge and asked him to increase my sentence so that I could stay in the jail. It was probably a very strange request, since most inmates are desperate to leave their prisons, but I was not the typical inmate, and my prison was inside my own head. The jail was the safest place for me. So I continued to live in my adopted home for the next several years, slowly healing from my wounds.

One year after Adil's kidnapping, the arrival of a new volunteer heralded a transformation. Her name was Rana and she was a retired therapist with decades of experience helping mentally unstable patients. Although I didn't enjoy being called unstable, I quickly became dependent on her. I cannot explain how much she helped me, dear reader; in fact, it would be safe to say that Rana saved my life. Over the course of the next two years, she visited me every week. In the most considerate and non-judgmental manner, she coaxed me out of my darkness and into the light.

When I didn't feel like talking, she spent the hours silently at my side. As I became more talkative, she asked me questions about my family, my work as a cook. She would often inquire about a recipe, or seek my advice about the best way to cook *biryani* or *shahi tukray*. She didn't think twice about hugging me when I felt sad or laughing with me over some joke. She discussed religion in a very sensible and nonjudgmental way, understanding why I had lost my faith, but encouraging me to find it again. When she discovered that I had attended the adult literacy center in the jail some time ago, she encouraged me to continue with my studies. I had thought that I lost my love of learning after Adil, but the books she brought me awakened my spirit once more. Poetry, literature, even history and geography – I devoured it all in an effort to fill the emptiness inside me. And, slowly, I recovered.

Although I loved all kinds of subjects, I found my passion to be writing. Once I attained the means to put down my thoughts on paper, I never looked back. Several times over the course of my therapy, Rana advised me to pen my biography. She believed it would give me closure and help me heal. For a long while I was afraid to take her advice, not sure of what the process would reveal. But as I explained to you at the beginning, dear reader, I made her a promise that I would try, and hence I started to write down my memories of the years past. As I did so, I realized that it was indeed having a therapeutic effect on me. It allowed me to think, even plan ahead. It helped me see how strong I was, how present the hand of Allah had been in my life all along. Writing about my past gave me hope for my future.

Other things, other people, also gave me confidence. The women's section of the jail is itself a beacon of hope for women like me, who have no one to turn to but strangers, in their darkest hour of need. In the last year of my self-imposed sentence I started to receive visitors again, as if my mental well-being had somehow communicated itself to them. My brothers came a few times with their wives, my sisters with their children. It was wonderful to feel part of a family once again, to feel loved and wanted.

Most surprisingly, my childhood friend Samreen visited me twice. She looked much older than her years; despite her father's wealth, life had not treated her kindly. She told me about an adulterous husband, an unfulfilled desire to have children. Perhaps because of her own tragedies, she felt the need to build bridges, re-examine old relationships. She told me that she forgave me for that imagined theft so many years ago. I didn't insist upon my innocence. I had learned that some things are best left in the past, and I truly pitied her. Imagine, reader, that a prisoner with a tragic past such as mine should pity a rich, young woman who seemed to have everything. Yet pity her I did, because she was, after all, also a prisoner of her own situation.

We spent the better part of the day chatting, slowly becoming friends again. Because I was not a traditional inmate, the regular rules of visiting hours were often waived for me. Samreen asked me about Adil, and the whole sordid tale came tumbling out of me as if we had never been apart. We talked hesitantly about Waseem and his role in my torture. She informed me that he had fallen out of favor with the police department and was unable to use his connections to protect himself any longer. Although he had left their home long ago, she promised to find out from her parents where he was living now, and to talk to her husband's brother who was a judge. Samreen, who had not crossed my mind even once for close to ten years, was the one person who gave me immense hope. Perhaps Adil was still alive, perhaps Waseem could be found and held accountable. Despite my disillusionment with the legal system, the dream was enough to heal me.

Today, I have completed my journal as promised. I have addressed it to you, Adil, my dearest reader, because I have hope that one day, with the help of Samreen, I will find you. After ten long and eventful years, I am finally leaving my adopted home with more than a little sadness. Ten years ago, when I arrived as a scared young woman at this unassuming jail I had no idea what lay ahead. Today I walk out a free woman at last; wounded but still standing, I don't know what will happen tomorrow. All I know is that I have had a good life; despite its tragedies, I've made some good friends, learned a lot about this world, and that, *inshallah* I will survive.

This journal will always be with me, so that one day if – no, when – I find you, you can read about my journey. Until then, my dearest reader, my beloved son, be safe wherever you are. My prayers are with you.

Glossary

(All words are in Urdu, Pakistan's official language, unless otherwise noted)

Aaloo gosht: a spicy dish made of potatoes (aaloo) and lamb, goat or cow meat (gosht).

Abba: father.

Alhamdolillah: a term meaning all praise to God (Arabic).

Allah: God (Arabic).

Ammi: mother.

Assalamo Alaikum: Islamic greeting meaning "peace be with you" (Arabic).

Baba: father.

Baji: older sister. May also be used by those of lower social status when addressing a young woman of higher status.

Beta: male child or son. Used by parents, as well as other elders when addressing those younger than themselves and at an equal social footing.

Beti: a female child or son.

Bibi: a young woman.

Biddat: innovation or new teachings/practices creeping into religion (Arabic).

Biryani: a spicy meat and rice dish.

Burqa: an enveloping outer garment worn by some Muslim women, especially in Afghanistan and the northern areas of Pakistan.

Chaat: a popular street food generally consisting of fruit, fried bread, yoghurt or chickpeas.

Chador: an outer garment or open cloak worn over the head and shoulders and held closed with the hands or wound around the upper body. A traditional form of covering for some Muslim women.

Chapatti: a very thin, unleavened flat bread eaten daily.

Charpoy: a woven bed consisting of a wooden frame bordering a set of ropes.

Daal: a thick stew prepared from a variety of dried lentils and spices. It is often eaten with plain white rice.

Dhabba: a roadside restaurant or truck stop serving local cuisine.

Dupatta: a long scarf-like fabric worn as part of the Pakistani dress. It can be worn several ways, including covering the head, draped over one shoulder, or tied around the waist. In some modern shalwar kameez outfits, the dupatta is absent.

Gori: a white girl or woman, generally denoting a European or American female.

Inshallah: if God wills it (Arabic).

Halwa: sweet confection made of a variety of ingredients.

Hashish: a drug made from cannabis, consumed by being hated in a pipe or other instrument.

Hijab: a specific type of religious headscarf worn by Muslim women in some parts of the world. Also signifies the overall concept of modesty maintained by them (Arabic).

Ji: when added to a word such as Sahib or Abba, a further term for respect and affection.

Kameez: a long tunic worn as part of the Pakistani dress. Designs vary in terms of tunic and sleeve length, neckline, and much more.

Khuda Hafiz: a popular form of goodbye, meaning may God be your protector.

Kurti: a short tunic in the style of a kameez but worn over jeans or pants.

Lakh: a unit in the Indian/Pakistani numbering system equivalent to 100,000.

Ma: mother.

Madrassah: an ancient school of religious or secular learning (Arabic). Currently may be a center for religious extremism in many countries.

Mashallah: a phrase implying appreciation, joy or thankfulness at good news or a happy event. Also used as a protection against jealousy or envy from others (Arabic).

Maulvi: a Muslim cleric.

Naan: a leaved, oven-baked flatbread.

Naat: a form of poetry that praises the Prophet Muhammad (Arabic). It may be sung or spoken.

Nani: maternal grandmother.

Pakora: a fried snack similar to a fritter, cooked by covering vegetables, meat or lentils in gram-flour batter and frying.

Paratha: a lightly pan-fried unleaved flatbread that may or may not be stuffed with filling such as onion, potatoes, minced meat and much more.

Pulao: a non-spicy rice pilaf dish which may consist of vegetables or meat.

Puri: deep fried bread.

Rabab: a type of string instrument used to play traditional folk tunes (Urdu/Arabic).

Ramadan: the holy month of fasting for Muslims (Arabic).

Sahib: boss or superior officer. Also used to signify any older person at a higher social or economic footing than the speaker.

Salaam: an abbreviated form of the traditional Islamic greeting, meaning peace (Arabic/Urdu).

Shami kabab: a small patty made of ground beef, egg and ground chickpeas. Eaten as a snack or with bread like naan or chapatti.

Shalwar: a loose pant worn as part of the Pakistani dress, both for males and females.

Sohan Halwa: a type of hard traditional dessert made of sugar, boiling milk and water, with pistachios and almonds added in.

Subhanallah: glorious is God (Arabic).

Shia: a follower of Shiite Islam, the second largest denomination of the religion.

Sufi: a follower of Sufism, a sect of Islam that focuses on mysticism and philosophy (Arabic).

Tabla: a pair of musical instruments similar to bongos, often played with traditional folk music.

Qawwali: a form of Sufi devotional music that has gained mainstream popularity in recent decades.

Wa alaikum assalam: the response to the Islamic greeting of "assalamo alaikum". It translates to "and peace be on you as well (Arabic).

Ya Allah: Oh my God! (Arabic).

Yaar: slang for friend, pal.